After the Border

43 Eye-Opening, Shocking, Crazy, Happy & Fun Stories from a Retired U.S. Immigration Officer

By Richard Lee

I would like to thank my dear friend Tom Yost – my pre-editor, sounding board and contributing writer; Julie Price from Priceless Digital Media, LLC, for formatting and helping to develop my project; and Cutting J. from Fiverr.com for editing my work. Without the help of these people this project would not have been completed.

Cover and interior design by Priceless Digital Media, LLC
www.PricelessDigitalMedia.com

Contents

Preface

In the intricate tapestry of American society, immigration has always been a vital thread woven into the nation's very fabric. It represents the pursuit of dreams, the quest for a better life, and the promise of new beginnings. Yet, within the luminous narrative of hope and opportunity, there exists a shadowy realm concealed beneath the surface, where deception and fraud lurk.

"After the Border: 43 Eye-Opening, Shocking, Crazy, Happy & Fun Stories from a Retired U.S. Immigration Officer" embarks on a journey into the hidden corners of the American immigration system, shedding light on the often obscured stories of individuals who manipulate this pathway for their own gain. It unravels the narratives of those who employ fraudulent marriages as a means to secure entry into the United States, exploiting the compassionate and welcoming nature of a nation built by immigrants.

This book is not just an exploration of immigration fraud; it is a testament to the resilience of the American spirit and the commitment to upholding the principles of justice, truth, and fairness. Through extensive research, personal accounts, and the insights of experts in immigration law, we delve into the complexities of this issue, seeking to understand the motivations behind such deceptions and the consequences they bring to individuals, families, and society as a whole.

As you turn the pages of "After the Border," you will encounter compelling stories of love turned sinister, visa applications tainted by dishonesty and the intricate web of laws and regulations designed to combat immigration fraud. You will also meet the dedicated professionals who work tirelessly to unveil these shadows, ensuring that the American dream remains attainable for those who seek it through legitimate means.

This book is a call to awareness and action, encouraging us all to examine the challenges and vulnerabilities within our immigration system. By shining a light on these shadows, we aim to foster a society that values integrity, compassion, and justice while still extending a welcoming hand to those who come to America in pursuit of their dreams.

"After the Border" invites you to explore a crucial aspect of the American experience—one that reveals the complexities, contradictions, and enduring ideals that shape the nation's ongoing immigration story.

Introduction
to Immigration

It is important to give you some understanding of immigration terms while you read this book. I'm not going to use a lot of legal terms or make this overly complex because this is not an immigration class. But you need to have some grasp of how immigration works and what terminology I'll often use. These stories are not for people with in-depth knowledge of immigration looking for an official tutorial. It's for everyone, including a few insights for immigration lawyers and immigration officers.

I'll talk about specific aspects of immigration, primarily fraud, and what occurs in immigration inside the United States. The big issue for most people is what's happening at the Mexican border. What's happening now? The first thing I want you to understand is what we know versus what you see in the media or political propaganda. The biggest number of illegal immigrants who come into this country do not come through the Mexican border. They come through the airports.

People from all over the world cross the southern border of the U.S. without processing. Without coming into a port of entry, an immigrant's status is both illegal and undocumented. People who come in through the airports come in legally and think of the airport as a giant port of entry. They have a visa to come here for the most part. Unless they lie and use someone else's name, they gain entry by going through U.S. Immigration and Customs.

The number we often hear is about 40 percent of illegal immigrants come through the Mexican border, so 60 percent of the rest come in through the airports. Why doesn't the northern border with Canada garner attention like the southern border? Most people cross into the U.S.

through the Canadian border with visas or visa waivers. Now, when I say Canada, a small pittance of people come here illegally through Canada. These are generally not Canadians, by the way. These are people who fly into Canada and then come into the U.S.

Why don't we talk about blocking the Canadian border? Because most people don't come here illegally and stay forever. A lot of Canadians come here on vacation in Florida while it's wintertime in Canada. Then they go home. Overwhelmingly, they go home. And most of them are retirees living on the beach a little longer than perhaps they should.

I want you to understand the two terms that we use. *Legal* and *illegal*, although now we would say *legal* and *undocumented*. This is a misnomer because lots of people come here with documents, but they're still in the country illegally: they overstayed their visa, they're working, they're taking jobs, they have no reason to be here, and they have no other status. Their status has expired, or they have taken a job when not authorized. They are illegal in the country.

You'll see immigration advocacy groups say, "No human is illegal." However, a person's immigration status and actions certainly can be illegal; therefore, you can illegally be in the country, an illegal alien, as defined by current law. *Illegal alien* means you're from a foreign country (alien), and your status and actions are operating outside of U.S. law (illegal). If you find this as a pejorative to immigrants, please feel free to change the law.

Some definitions:

- *Undocumented* people cross the border illegally. They come into this country without documents. They don't go through Customs and Border Patrol for Inspection and to be admitted legally.

- *Documented and illegal-status immigrants* are people who came in with B-2 visitor visas and student visas, as examples. They were supposed to go home and never left, and so they are illegally in the country.

- *Immigrants* are people who've applied to come to this country permanently. These are husbands, wives, sons, daughters, mothers, fathers, brothers, and sisters of U.S. citizens. These are also husbands, wives, and children of legal permanent residents. They are coming into this country to live in this country permanently. What this means is they've filed for their paperwork while they were overseas at a U.S. visa location in their homeland to come into the country. Some people start the process by filing as an employee of a U.S. company and come here to stay in a lengthier process.

- *Nonimmigrants* come here for a multitude of reasons. You have diplomats who come here as nonimmigrants. You have people who work for other government agencies; I will share more details about that later. You have people who come here as temporary workers, seasonal workers, and day-pass workers. You may have heard of H-1Bs and things of that nature. Some of the nonimmigrants are workers who come here temporarily, and some of them can change their immigrant status.

- I'm not going to go into every one of the visa codes because it's enormous, and that would be more than necessary; however, in some of the stories, I'll show techniques that are used in systemic immigration fraud that involve corporate manipulation, and that exploit government apathy.

- People primarily come to the U.S. as a nonimmigrant to visit. They come here as *B-2 visa visitors* and sometimes *B-1 visitors*. B-1s are employment visitors. They're coming here for something related to business. They're not coming here to work.

- *Student F-1 visas* are for foreigners studying in U.S. colleges.

- People come here for training or as *J-1 students*, or people who come in here to work in special youth camps (camp counselors), things like that. J-1s come for summer programs to learn about hospitality. They're coming here for job training. That's short-term. People come to the U.S. as *M-1;* they're like F-1 students, but they're coming here for specific practical training. Think of the 9/11 terrorists. One came in on a temporary student visa, like an F-1. One of the four pilot hijackers entered with a flight school training-specific visa, and the rest were six-month visitor visas. Unfortunately, they abused our system and significantly attacked our country.

In regard to the nonimmigrant categories, the majority of people who adjust their status or become legal permanent residents in the country are in the nonimmigrant category when they first arrive. Then, they find some means to change their status to become an immigrant. This is generally by marriage, sometimes, the attempted status upgrade is employment-based.

The important distinctions are between the immigrant who is coming here to live permanently and the nonimmigrant who is coming here temporarily. When talking about illegal aliens who cross the border, they're not documented at all and don't fit into the two main categories.

Other terms that we use are *legal permanent residents*. Think of the movie *Green Card* or think of the green card itself. You've heard of it. Most people understand the green card concept. This is a legal permanent resident, someone who has immigrated to the country. The first thing you get is the legal permanent status or conditional status. Many people who marry get conditional status. It's only good for two years. At the end of two years, they apply to get that condition removed, and they become a legal permanent resident forever. A year after that, if it's marriage-based, conditional residents can file for U.S. citizenship, so after three years they can get U.S. citizenship.

Others who come here as immigrants not married to U.S. citizens have to wait five years to become U.S. citizens. We call this process *naturalization*. They file a form N-400 to apply for citizenship, and once that's approved, they go to a ceremony where they're sworn in as U.S. citizens, with all the rights and privileges of any U.S. citizen. I've been to many of these ceremonies; they're quite moving and emotional at times.

When it comes to citizenship, we have *citizenship by birth, citizenship by blood*, and *citizenship through naturalization*. Those are three different ways you get citizenship. If you're born in this country, then you're a U.S.

citizen. If your parents are U.S. citizens and you were born outside of the country, you're a U.S. citizen. If you come as a legal permanent resident, you can be naturalized as a U.S. citizen after five years, or a faster three-year period if married to a U.S. citizen.

We'll talk about some of the forms that are used in immigration. I don't want to go deeply into those, but some of the basic forms are important to piece the immigration puzzle together.

- The I-485 *application to adjust status* is important. This form is used for immigrants who are already in the United States. They can fill out the form to become a legal permanent resident if they meet certain requirements.

- *I-130 petition for an alien relative.* This is a petition that's filed by U.S. citizens and legal permanent residents who want a family member to either come into the country or is in the country and wants them to become a legal permanent resident.

- *I-751.* If they've been married for two years, they file that form to remove the conditional legal permanent resident status.

- The next way people become permanent residents is for employers (companies) to file for the immigrant worker to stay.

- *N-400 form* for people who wish to become U.S. citizens. Just know that there are lots of people who are legal permanent residents but never become citizens.

- *N-600 form.* That's an application parents file for their children to become citizens. These children often were not citizens at birth but are eligible for citizenship through their parents. Generally, children of U.S. citizens living abroad are coming to this country to get the child's citizenship acknowledged. It is complicated, but we will discuss this later. Some foreign-adopted children may use this method as well.

I've got great real-life stories addressing these terms and issues that are fun, sad, shocking, tender, and some that will make your blood boil. Enjoy!

Harvey Tipler

I want to take a moment to tell a story that is a little bit different. It does have an immigration kick to it, which I hope you find interesting.

In 1994, I was working for U.S. Senator Richard **Shelby** (at the time a Democrat). I was a field representative for him and traveled around South Alabama.

A friend of mine who worked for Senator Howell **Heflin** (the other U.S. Senator from Alabama) introduced me to a gentleman named Harvey Tipler. We all went out for drinks when I was in D.C. at one time. Harvey was a charismatic, attractive man. Women gravitated to him. He was also from a wealthy family.

The next time I met Harvey was in Alabama. As a field representative, you spend a good deal of your time on the road. I would travel throughout South Alabama meeting mayors, council members, and state and local politicians. I also spent a bit of time meeting prominent businessmen and lawyers. Harvey's family had a lucrative legal firm in Andalusia, Alabama. I was always encouraged to stop by and see Harvey. His father had started their law firm and had grown to have offices in Los Angeles, London and a few other cities.

I like to talk about what it means to be alive and how we should treat others. It is always interesting to have thoughtful conversations. Also, you can learn a lot about someone through these types of conversations.

I like to think this perspective helps me read people. As we sat talking, I said to Harvey, "I think it's important when people have done something wrong, they should feel a sense of guilt. A guilty conscience can help us improve our behavior."

I saw it as part of the process for the mind to help us recognize wrong and not act that way again: a pathway to becoming a better person. We need an internal ethical code to keep us in check. We all break that moral code at some point in time. The difference that separates us is that, as decent human beings, we feel guilty when we do something wrong, and everyone does something wrong at some point in time. This was the gist of our conversation.

During that conversation, Harvey said to me, "I never feel guilty for anything I do." He was matter of fact about it, crystal clear.

Later, I would learn a few personal things about Harvey that would back that statement up. I cannot go into detail, and it was secondhand hearsay. I believe those stories had some truth to them. The publicly known events about Harvey Tipler are equally shocking and sad.

There was some indication from people that knew Harvey that he had some desire to run for politics or be governor of Alabama one day. I never thought politics suited him; he did appear to have the ego for it. Harvey Tipler's name sounded equally fitting for a Charles Dickens novel or an Alabama governorship.

Now, the salary of the governor at the time was about $46,000 a year. Harvey let everyone know he spent about $50,000 a month. That was on his personal expenses. He was proud of the fact that he did that. Now, I do not begrudge anyone for their wealth. I am not one of these people who thinks people who are wealthy are inherently evil or don't deserve their money. People generally work hard for their money. They deserve it.

But I am concerned about people who have no conscience whatsoever. As I said, I don't remember all of the conversations we had, but I distinctly remember his lack of morality. I met a friend of mine who had introduced me to Harvey. The first thing I said to this gentleman was, "I think at some point Harvey Tipler is going to go to prison."

My friend looked at me, surprised, and said, "No, Harvey is a great guy. He's a wonderful guy."

I kind of shrugged and said, "OK, maybe I'm wrong."

I didn't think I was wrong to think he was headed to the Big House, but you know, I placated my friend. I tell that story because when you read the history of Harvey Tipler, and I look back on talking with my friend about Harvey, our conversation became extremely revealing.

Fast-forward to twenty years later. I was at my U.S. Immigration office in Atlanta. I was actually in the lunchroom with one of my colleagues and shared this story about Harvey Tipler and my time working for Senator Shelby.

As I was talking about this in the lunchroom with some of my other colleagues, I hadn't mentioned any names yet. I was talking about Andalusia, and this older gentleman, this attorney, and one of my colleagues piped up, and he said, "I know exactly whom you're talking about. You're talking about Harvey Tipler. He is my cousin."

Insert sound effects when the record stops with the screeching sound: uh-oh. Needless to say, I was a bit embarrassed and concerned I might have offended him.

He then said to me, "Harvey is going to prison."

So this man gave me the basic skinny stories I did not know. I won't share those because they are family-focused.

But the publicly reported stories are as fascinating.

Harvey was representing a young lady who happened to be a stripper working at one of the clubs in South Alabama. The story goes that he was trying to force her to perform sex acts. This was because she could not afford his legal fees. He was an expensive attorney. She was not happy about this and ended up going to the Alabama State Bar. This was a multiyear investigation and process. However, he eventually got disbarred from the states of Alabama and California. Now unable to practice law, Harvey Tipler attempted to get a legal license in South Carolina. When that failed, Harvey moved to Florida and was still eligible to practice law in the state of Florida, but he hadn't taken the bar exam.

My understanding from reading the newspaper clippings and speaking to his cousin was that Harvey decided to practice immigration law. It turned out he was not really practicing immigration law. He did advertisements to do immigration law and apparently took upwards of $200,000 from individuals to file immigration paperwork. Apparently, he never ended up filing any immigration paperwork for anyone. Obviously, Harvey wasn't allowed to represent them because he wasn't part of the Florida State Bar.

This is really a damning note about the legal system in the United States and particularly the American Bar Association. The system is supposed to oversee these really corrupt attorneys, and there are tons of them. Harvey is a great example of this inept system. He kept doing this stuff or other unethical behavior.

Because of what he was doing with immigrants, he ended up being incarcerated. While he was in jail awaiting trial, Harvey conspired with someone to kill the U.S. district attorney who was prosecuting him. Apparently, there was quite a bit of evidence. Harvey was convicted and sentenced to thirty years in prison. In all the crimes that Harvey Tipler was involved with, including immigration fraud and attempting to have a young lady perform sexual acts for him, none of this got him a lengthy prison term. The system had to wait until he tried to kill another attorney.

What's the moral of that story? As you will read from my other stories, there's a raging debate in the U.S. and in my conscience about crime and punishment, especially regarding morals, ethics, and norms as it pertains to immigration.

The life of Harvey Tipler didn't have a happy ending similar to Ebenezer Scrooge from Charles Dickens's *Christmas Carol,* with the ghosts of Christmas past, present, and future aligning Harvey's moral compass. There's so much to unpack in Harvey's story, especially the larger picture: sex crimes against U.S. citizens go unnoticed; abuse of immigrants raises only legal eyebrows; and the real force of the law was thrust upon Harvey when he broke rank with the legal continuum to harm one of his professional kin.

The legal system will protect lawyers to the best of their ability. Yeah, it might disbar them. But it'll disbar them for things that you and I as individuals would go to prison for in a heartbeat. Because of their Power and Influence, they get off the hook all the time, but in an ethical system, they should be sent to jail first, not last, especially as officers of the court.

If you would like to read more about Harvey Tipler, search the web.

Challenges for
Immigration Officers

The ending of the prior scenario would not happen in most places today because in many instances, you can't even get Homeland Security Investigations to come into the office to arrest people. After all, my own branch of U.S. Immigration (USCIS) does not utilize Homeland Security Investigations. In some offices in California, HSI Agents have been blocked from entering USCIS offices. I mean, it's not that bad that no one gets in, but you have to jump through some serious hoops to rightfully arrest and deport anyone anymore. We were supposed to have this arm of government (Homeland Security Investigations) take care of U.S. Immigration (USCIS) and help us with criminal investigations, and that's not the case.

USCIS does everything it can to block Homeland Security investigations. I'll give you a story that was relayed to me by my friends with Homeland Security Investigations (HSI). Again, I worked closely with HSI for ten years, and we did a lot of cases. I knew Homeland Security guys from all over the country.

I also knew FDNS (Fraud Detection and National Security) officers who were in the San Bernardino area working in the offices of USCIS. And I'll tell you the story that was relayed to me about that. When Syed Rizwan Farook and Tashfeen Malik, a married couple, attacked and shot up the Christmas party, Homeland Security Investigations, FBI and the State Department went to USCIS California to look at their immigration files to review for criminal investigation on these individuals and any accomplices at large. The director of the USCIS office in California blocked HSI from coming into the office and did everything she could to interfere with the investigation, which she was not supposed to do. The USCIS California director was extremely belligerent toward the investigators after this horrific crime occurred. This is the way the story was told to me by fellow Homeland Security members.

The investigators had to jump through enormous hoops to get the files from these immigrants who had died committing a terrorist act. Under the law and under the rules and regulations, when Homeland Security or any investigative agency is doing a criminal investigation, we are supposed to help them. We're supposed to work with them. This Director did not do that. She did everything she could not do. The Director of California USCIS was reprimanded for this, but in the end, this particular individual was promoted up the food chain and moved to the California Service Center. There, she could manage a great number of immigrant filings. This is the story that was told to me; however, I have no doubt about it at all. I worked for this agency for twenty years and saw this type of activity. They do this.

I had to work with our own head of the legal department many times on criminal court cases. And one lawyer in the Atlanta office constantly put us through obstacles. By hindering any type of investigation type of work, her sole job seemed to be to ensure that investigations were as limited as possible. I don't think the counsel was a bad person. I think the counsel was being directed from headquarters and told the rules and guidelines that were set forth. It's all under the guise of protecting USCIS.

This was a sham from the top. I can tell you from personal experience how frustrating it was working with the U.S. attorney's Office, especially when my own U.S. Immigration chief counsel wasn't expediting the process. I got cases that should obviously be prosecuted, and some cases weren't necessarily mine. U.S. attorneys had to fight with our chief counsel (USCIS) to get information.

It was always a battle. The U.S. Attorney's Office would tell you that it was frustrating and difficult to work with USCIS, and they didn't have any other agency that caused them as many problems as USCIS Administration and its legal team.

Introduction to Marriage Fraud

There are three basic types of marriage fraud. Each type of marriage fraud can branch out to more complex schemes. There are single-scheme marriages, single scheme one-sided marriages, and finally arranged fraudulent marriages.

First, we have something called the *single scheme* marriage fraud. Single scheme marriages are two people conspiring with each other and not being honest about their marriage motives or details. This is where you see the U.S. citizen receiving money from the Immigrant or just the USC is a friend and wants to help. Friendship marriages are hard to prove as fraudulent. The USC friend does not receive any compensation for the marriage. With a lot of the single schemes, you suspect that it's fraudulent. If they're friends, they know a lot about each other. So when you ask them questions, when you delve into marriage and as two human beings interacting, single-scheme couples have a great deal of information about each other. You suspect that it's a bad marriage, but there's not a lot you can do about it.

I didn't like investigating friendship single-scheme cases. It wasn't something I was fond of doing; both people involved were decent people, one trying to help the other out. Now, there was one case in which I didn't mind finding fraud. I was glad to uncover it for one simple reason: it involved a police officer who worked for one of the police departments in Georgia. He had married a friend of his. The girl that he married was one of his best friends.

His supposed spouse was an Eastern European lady living with another man from her home country. The two Eastern Europeans had overstayed the permitted entry, and they needed to go home. They didn't want to stay in their home country, so the police officer agreed to marry the female so that she could stay. The problem was that he was a police officer, and I don't care what your reason is behind circumventing the law. As an officer, you've sworn an oath to uphold the law and the Constitution.

If the couple had gone to their home country in Eastern Europe, they would not be in any danger. They lived a good lifestyle in their home country. There were no threats to them. I would have loved for them to stay—nice people—but there were legal ways that they could have stayed. With the assistance of my report, Homeland Security Investigations (HSI) determined the police officer's marriage to the Eastern European immigrant was fraudulent. Instead of prosecuting the police officer, HSI presented the evidence to the certification board for police in the state of Georgia. The board revoked the police officer's certificate, and he lost his job. He may never be an officer again. The Eastern European immigrants' visa waivers expired, and they went home.

This is typical of people who were empathetic and wanted to help someone they went to school with. For example, a young girl from Iowa married a guy to help him stay here. He was from an African country. She wanted to help him stay, so she married him. They never lived together nor spent a day in the same house together. She was in Iowa, and he was in Atlanta, but they went to college together, so she married him. She stuck with her story about their marriage. She was in it for him, and I understood she thought what she was doing was genuinely the right thing to do.

I also feel empathy for the immigrants who do this, and I understand why they do it. My concern is that they don't understand the danger that they're putting everyone in by getting away with this. Bad people learn how to play the game, and a fraud technique can grow exponentially. How do you tell another person what they did was wrong when you did it yourself? No one is above the law, but not many people follow it, including the government, which is apathetic to prosecuting immigration marriage fraud cases.

Single Scheme
One-sided Fraud

The other single scheme that we see is called *single scheme one-sided fraud* or second type of marriage fraud. This is more common than both spouses in a single-scheme fraud. This is one of the fraud scams U.S. Immigration sees all the time: the U.S. citizen meets some immigrant and falls in love with him or her. Then, the U.S. citizen petitions for the immigrant and helps them get legal residence. Often, the U.S. citizen is in it to win it, as I like to say; they're head over heels in love with this person.

It's hard to have an honest, open discussion with people. We're not used to it. We're not built for it. I often say, "If you can't meet a 10 in the United States (referencing the Bo Derek movie *10*, where a normal nerdy guy meets a supermodel on a scale of 1 to 10, *10* being the best), shouldn't you be suspicious?" To the U.S. citizen gunning for a marriage visa: "You're pulling that male or female supermodel from another part of the world? I'm suspicious of that relationship." I say that with trepidation. I'm not overwhelmingly attractive. I'm not Brad Pitt. But I'm rational and reasonable enough to know if Angelina Jolie is hitting on me and wants to wed or bed me, I'm going to be a little bit suspicious. *Why the heck is she after me? I'm Joe Blow.* It's kind of like when people win the lottery. They spent thirty years never having a model attracted to them, they win $100 million, and all of a sudden, they have ten *10s* chasing them down. Did their physical features change? Their personality? No, but their money changed, or the benefit changed.

This is the same thing with immigration. You see an unattractive man with a stunningly beautiful woman. I mean, unattractive men, not even wealthy. The thing they have to offer is a legal status that is a valuable commodity across the world, more than most U.S. citizens realize. Many U.S. citizens who petition or sponsor beautiful immigrants don't have any money; they don't drive a nice car. Some of them live in trailers. You see, sometimes these are attractive women who are well dressed. You can see that they're used to a certain standard of living. But these guys think that they've won the jackpot. You get to see them when they first get married. They filed their immigration paperwork. They follow the I-751 (obtaining status through marriage) process to get their conditions removed. Then, they file an N-400 (application for naturalization) to become citizens, usually for three years. Somewhere in that process, nearly all of those marriages fail.

As soon as they get their legal permanent resident status, that beautiful, attractive woman is gone. That beautiful, attractive man is gone. Sometimes, as soon as they get married and start the immigration process, she's filing an I-360 petition, claiming the male is a batterer.

The reason I know this is I saw them through the entire process. I saw the immigrants coming in after obtaining status (green card or citizenship), often returning to an original spouse from their home country. Now, filing for that old spouse to get benefits.

The beginning of the lengthy process in marriage fraud is divorcing one's actual wife from one's home country. This opens the door to a green card through a gullible U.S. citizen seduced by the newly divorced immigrant. All the filings that they do for the immigration and foreign marriage process are designed to remove the home country spouse, marry the American, then dump the American after obtaining immigration status, remarrying their original spouse from your home country.

I also got complaints from U.S. citizens who were dejected and devastated after being used and defrauded. The guy follows her through the process for two years. His wife gets permanent residence, and she leaves within a week. He's calling us up, saying, "She left me as soon as she got her legal permanent resident status. She left me the day after she got citizenship. I think she married me to get citizenship."

That happens a lot—way too often. And there's little an officer can do about it because they've gone through the process. I asked them in the beginning, "Is this a good marriage?" I allowed them to prove, disprove, or share their doubts in the U.S. Immigration vetting process, and they usually stick to the marriage route, only to learn the real motives of their immigrant spouse after the paperwork has cleared and the status is given. At that point, it's too late for the U.S. citizen, and the manipulative spouse is gone.

In another strange twist, some Americans who are taken in already know this. They know what's going on—that they're being used—and they're happy with it.

I like to tell the story of a U.S. citizen who came in, a little nerdy guy, not attractive. He was married to an Eastern European girl who was stunningly beautiful. We talked to him about the marriage, and we talked to him about some of the issues we saw. I remember him being asked about the marriage and whether it was good.

This guy looked at the officer and he said, "Have you looked at this woman?"

"Yes," the officer replied.

The man said, "Do you see how gorgeous she is?"

The officer replied, "Yeah."

The guy said, "I'm sleeping with her every night. If it ends in two years, it ends in two years. But I'm having the time of my life."

As an immigration officer, what can you do with that? That filing was approved.

I guess until our U.S. citizen gets kicked off *Survivor* Foreign Marriage Island, our fellow citizen definitely lives by the Latin phrase *carpe diem*, or seize the day. Or in this case, *carpe momenta priusquam relinquit* ... seize the moments before she leaves. And our guy could care less if she dumped him down the road. The U.S. citizen with the beautiful immigrant wife proved beyond a reasonable doubt that he regularly consummated the marriage ... and so was immediately stamped for approval by U.S. Immigration.

In these single-scheme one-sided fraud cases, I'm not talking about the U.S. citizen being involved in marriage fraud. I'm talking about those who were fooled into getting into these marriages from love, lust, or the mystique of foreign fiancées. I saw the heartbreak that many of these U.S. citizens go through when they've been used that way. People get used all the time in different ways. It happens a lot. Most people, men, and women, are heartbroken and financially broken. There is not much the courts, or the lawyers will do.

Immigration officers always want to get the U.S. citizens to stop and see the big picture; blinded by love, almost everyone goes through with the marriage and gets booted as soon the immigrant gets the status they want.

I have talked about men, but this happens to women a lot more often. Women end up with these guys who are extremely attractive, well-educated, and capable of making a lot of money. The foreign groom swoons the woman and promises her the moon. She's often uneducated, and not attractive, but this guy wants her ... it's true love! You'd be shocked at how often the same women come in after the marriage and immigration process and complain. "He never touched me or wanted to have sex with me."

I've seen it in the romantic victim's eyes. I've talked to them after they've gone through the pain and trauma after they've been used. They've been devastated by the fact that he only used me for the green card. Often when you talk to them, they know that this doesn't make sense. "But he's so charismatic. He's so attentive." But female U.S. citizens do it anyway, like male U.S. citizens. I'm not sure that I wouldn't be any different, you know if I was lonely and saw a beautiful woman come at me with full charm. Who's to say that I wouldn't fall for the same trap?

AIDS For Everyone

From 2004 to 2011, we (immigration officers) saw a lot of West Africans and South Africans coming into the country who were HIV positive. These individuals married U.S. citizens, and the U.S. citizens applied for benefits for them.

This happened frequently. Every officer in Atlanta had this happen on a weekly basis, oftentimes a daily occurrence, a case once a week, or sometimes two or three times a week. From 2004 to 2008, I was an adjudications officer directly involved in that process and adjudicated these cases: granting them or denying them. Rest assured, in the Atlanta office, we discussed this issue as officers. I'm sorry for the long dialogue, but it's important for me to make sure and emphasize the importance of the issue.

Oftentimes, West African and South African males, along with South African women, would come in with HIV. But this is the typical story, one of many stories that I ran into. I had a West African male come into the immigration office. As I reviewed his case and started the adjudication process, I looked at his medical records. Now, mind you, every applicant who comes into the office must submit an I-693 medical exam for adjustment of status. On that medical exam, they must list any medical conditions they have. INS has different ranking types; for example, "Class A medical" have hepatitis. Maybe they have not taken all their shots for immunization. We must make sure that they're medically sound to be in the country, for the most part. During this time, immigrants needed proof they were HIV negative; a HIV positive test could bar the applicant from coming into the country and staying in the country. Mind you, with anything in INS, there's always a waiver; you can waive that HIV status in certain instances. And I'm not going to go into the overwhelming legal issues with waivers and all that stuff, but I'm going to give you the basics of it. For HIV personnel, they had to be able to prove that they were being medically treated or had been medically counseled for HIV, making sure they knew and were aware of what the issues were with HIV and AIDS.

This West African male came into the country and married an African American female. This is common. I reviewed the case, and he's HIV positive; he presents evidence that he's gone to the local clinic, usually the county office or some medical facility, and got counseling or observation that he was being treated and counseled. He's married to a U.S. citizen, an African-American woman. And so you ask them questions about their relationship. Some of the standard questions that we asked were discussed with the immigration officers. We frequently asked, "Hey, are you guys planning on having children?"

And inevitably, the African American woman almost always said, "Yes, we're planning on having kids."

The West African man would always say, "No, I'm not planning on having kids because of HIV."

I separated the husband and wife during the interview. One was sitting outside, and the other was speaking to me at my desk. You don't want to ask these questions when they're together. And I would always ask the West African man, I would say something like, "Have you told your spouse that you have HIV?"

All the time, the men would respond, "No, I have not told her."

I got this answer so frequently it was ridiculous: no, she has no idea that I am HIV positive. And the man would say something like, "Please, don't tell her that I have HIV; it will ruin my marriage."

And I would ask, "Are you using any type of contraceptive? Are you using protection?"

And every time, the man would say, "Yes, I'm using condoms."

And so, when I separated them, I would let him go outside and I would ask the African American female, "Do you use any kind of protection, or are you trying to get pregnant?"

Every time, the woman would say, we don't use any protection. We're trying to have kids, we want to have a baby together.

And I would point toward the male outside, "So you don't use condoms or birth control of any type?"

And she would say, "No, we don't use anything. We're trying to get pregnant."

So, we would often discuss these cases with fellow officers, and we would not discuss them in a way where we talked about the individuals themselves or gave out names or anything like that because we're not allowed to do that. We could talk about the issues in general. Each of us would be aghast. So, we would waive the fact that the individual had HIV and was not letting his or her spouse know. We were not allowed as officers to tell the U.S. citizen her husband is HIV positive. We are supposed to be protecting U.S. citizens, but we could not under the law disclose that she is married to a man who has HIV. She's sleeping with a man who has HIV, and they're not using protection. Mind you, during this time in Georgia, we had the highest rate of African American female infection with HIV. It was rampant in the Georgia area. We knew this was going on, and we were by law not allowed to tell these women that these men had HIV.

This is disgusting; it's unbelievable. When we raise this up the food chain to the higher-ups, they would tell us not to worry about it; that's not our business. Our business is to protect Americans—but that's not whom we protected.

It was around this time that we got word from the CDC that HIV was no longer a serious concern for the immigrants coming into this country. The policies came in during the Obama Administration, within a year or two, and said we should no longer be concerned about HIV. And it was no longer a thing that would require a waiver or to be concerned about. I will tell you that hands down, every officer that I talked to was shocked by this. We could not believe that the CDC, our government agency, had abandoned African American women in a time when African American women were getting HIV at a faster rate than any other group. We thought they didn't care.

- I would bring them back together at the end of the interview, and I would give them instructions. I would tell the applicant, "You have some medical issues and need to go back to your doctor." I would give them a letter requesting specific information. I would give it to the immigrant. Hopefully, I made the U.S. citizen aware that there was a serious medical issue that he or she needed to be concerned about. Maybe they would probe deeper. Maybe it would help them. I had to try and do this in a way that I would not get in trouble. I felt that it was a risk worth taking to try to at least give them some hint that this was extremely dangerous.

Hanging Out on I-285

I discussed early the concept of one-sided immigration fraud and what we mean by one-sided marriage fraud. You find that people are sometimes fooled into believing that a marriage is good. Sometimes, people are desperate for love. These are often the people who are easily fooled. I have seen so many broken hearts where people genuinely believed it was love, no matter how many bad signs. They could not be convinced otherwise until it hit them square in the face.

When I first started, I was interviewing a couple. The woman had bad hygiene and was a heavy smoker. During our conversation, she admitted to having low self-esteem. She was so happy to have found a husband.

Her husband was West African. He was attractive, well-dressed, and well-spoken. She thought he was in it for love, but in our conversation, you could tell she had doubts. Still, she was hopeful that she had won.

I interviewed them. Separated them and tried to determine if this marriage was legitimate. The U.S.spouse was adamant about the marriage and the fact that she loved him. I did not doubt that. Still, I did my best to see what kind of flaws there were. Maybe I was missing something.

What I learned is that they stayed apart during most weeks. He worked out of town and came home every other weekend. She understood and made the case that a lot of married couples have this arrangement. She admitted they had been intimate in the past, but not as much as she would like. When I finished the interview, I congratulated them, approved his permanent residence, and escorted them out the door. The female seemed a bit disturbed that I had questioned them at length about the marriage.

As we went out the door, she asked for a business card and suggested she might contact my supervisor. I gave her my card and sent them on their way. I figured at some point I would hear about the complaint.

This was around 10 a.m. I went to lunch after the interview. When I returned, I received a call from the same woman. There was a great deal of background noise. She was crying and a bit hysterical. When I was able to talk and get her calmed down, she told me the story. After getting his legal residence that morning, the husband headed home. Somewhere on Interstate I-285, the perimeter around Atlanta, he decided to pull over and let her out of the car right on the interstate.

She told me he shoved her out of the car. He told her he had his green card and no longer needed her. So, he left her on the side of a busy interstate.

I passed the information on to fraud. As a Service Officer, I had closed the case. It had approved him. Based on her testimony. I could not just reverse that decision on the spot. Having spoken to local counsel, they recommended doing nothing more.

He Fooled Me Twice

One more of these little single-scheme marriages. In this case, you have the same MO. An African American U.S. citizen married a West African man. In this case, I went out with one of my partners, who was with Homeland Security Investigations. We arrived as usual, early in the morning. This was a fourplex, two-story building. So, you had two apartments downstairs and two apartments upstairs.

There were no numbers on the doors. So, we weren't sure which apartment was the right one. What we suspected was that it was upstairs because the address started with two, and with most apartments, if it's two, it's an upstairs; if it's one, it's downstairs. We had to guess if the apartment was an odd number or an even number. *Is it on the right or the left?* We decided to flip a coin and knock on a door. We knocked on the door to the right. An elderly African-American woman opened the door. We showed our credentials and explained who we were and who we were there to see. She pointed us across the hall. We had knocked on the wrong door. The other door was the one we were looking for.

We knocked on the other door, and an African American we were looking for. You can kind of peek in the door a little bit, and we noticed that there was a mattress on the floor in the living room. A West African man showed up behind her a few seconds later, so they were both standing at the door. It was the couple we were looking for.

We spoke for a few minutes and asked a couple of basic questions. The African man was quiet. He was a little reserved. The African-American woman was a chatty Cathy. She liked to talk, smiling. She's friendly. Her demeanor made me think this was a good marriage. I didn't see any reason to do anything more. Let's face it, they're both in the house together. They're sleeping in the same house together.

I start to thank her and tell her I think everything is OK, and she interrupts me and encourages us to come into the house for a few minutes. She is almost adamant, and there is something in her voice that makes us both agree.

We enter the living room. The kitchen is right behind the living room as you walk in. It's a wide-open space. We notice that there is a couch as we go in the door to the right, and there's a mattress in front of the couch. On one end of the couch, there are bags of clothes. On the floor next to the bed is a suitcase.

I can't tell whether someone is moving in or someone is getting ready to move out. There are also a couple of bags in the kitchen. They appear to be bags of clothes.

I always want to be safe when I go into someone's house. I asked, "Hey, is there anyone else in the house?"

The lady tells me that her daughter, who's a young teenager, I think she might have been twelve or thirteen years old, is sleeping in one of the bedrooms. I asked to get a tour of the apartment so I could feel safe and make sure there was no one else in there.

She immediately agreed that was a great idea, and she asked the African man to give me a tour. The African man takes me to the next bedroom. It's down a little hall to the right. We go into the bedroom, I notice it's a setup somewhere between a man cave and a bedroom. In the closet are all his clothes. There's a lounge chair in there, there's a TV, what looks like a video game console, and there's a chest of drawers. It's set up like someone stays in there a lot. But there is no bed in the room.

He tells me this is his personal space where he gets away from everything and he gets to relax. It seems a little strange because it's not set up as a bedroom; it's set up as a living area. There is nothing in this room that would indicate that the woman ever spent any time in there. No female clothes, no female items on the dresser, nothing feminine whatsoever.

I ask if they can at least crack the door to let me see the room where the daughter is sleeping. He agrees to crack the door. It looked like she was sleeping in there. There is no one else in there. You do feel a little uncomfortable about opening a door where people are sleeping, but you also don't want to open a door and see there are fifteen people in the room.

We go back to the kitchen and the living room area. When we return, my partner looks at me and goes, "Well, I think we've got everything we need to know here, so let's let them get back to their lives.

I didn't see anything wrong up to this point. She seems a little overly friendly. And there's a nervous twitch, but not much. I'm getting the vibe that something doesn't fit, but you don't know what it is, right?

When we got back to the car, my partner then explained to me what was going on. When I took the African man out of the room, it allowed her to talk to the agent by herself. She had told the agent that the marriage was not good and she needed to speak with us privately. She told my partner that he was going to go to work soon, so this would give her time to call us back, or we could call her back, and she'd given her number to him.

This is the story she gave when we called her back. She was originally from North Carolina and had met him there years ago. I don't remember the exact circumstances, but they dated years prior; and they had broken it off. He had moved to Atlanta, and they lost touch over time.

She had not heard from him for years, and then, out of the blue, he contacted her again. She thought it was a little bit strange. I guess for her, there were some alarm bells lightly ringing. She had a really good job in North Carolina. She made good money. She was a little bit lonely and decided to give it a shot. They dated for a brief period while he was in Atlanta and she was in North Carolina, and they would see each other when they could.

He convinced her to quit her job and move down to Atlanta. They married, and she moved her daughter down here into the apartment with him. She did not know his immigration status when they were dating and when they got married. She always thought that he was legal and everything was copacetic. As soon as they got married, though, he explained to her that he did not have any legal status here and that they needed to file paperwork so he could stay for work and be a legal resident. She was perturbed that he had not told her this ahead of time and that this was kind of a last-minute thing. But in her mind, they were married, and as dutiful wives, she agreed to help him file immigration paperwork.

The problems began immediately in their relationship. Not just the fact that she didn't know about his immigration status, but once she filed the paperwork and once they had the interview, she said he became distant almost immediately. She said that the arrangement in the apartment was not as it appeared. She slept in the living room. She said he slept in the extra bedroom in the recliner. She said they never had sex. He was never at home for the most part, except to sleep. She was mad because she had left a good job in North Carolina to marry him. She couldn't find a good job in Atlanta.

She said the neighbor that we talked to earlier had caught him out in the parking lot in his pickup truck one day with another girl. They were making out. He treated her daughter poorly, and she was afraid for her. She felt trapped. She had nowhere to go. She had no money. She was stuck here with him.

I asked her to come into the office, and I would take a sworn statement from her. She agreed to meet me, and I took down everything she told me earlier with a lot more detail. I let her know that she had the right to withdraw the petition she had filed for him. She was concerned about that because she didn't know how he would react when her petition was withdrawn, especially if it came to her living arrangements.

We agreed to let her withdraw. She withdrew it in the office itself. I gave her a letter acknowledging that she had withdrawn her petition for him. I was able to convince the USCIS office and the immigration officers to hold off on denying his application to give her time to find a place to stay. I was concerned that he would throw her out of the apartment, and then she would be on her own with her young daughter or something worse.

The challenge with being an immigration service officer is you can't tell people, *hey, you need to go and see this agency, and they can help you.* When you're dealing with nonprofits and private institutions, you can't do that. The agency doesn't want you to appear to be favorable toward one institution over another. And I didn't readily have a list of community resources for her. I suggested that she could look up some help online.

I gave her my information. I told her that if I could help her, I would be glad to, and she could call me at any time, and we would do what we could to find some more resources. I don't think he threatened her. I mean, she had been a security guard. She looked like a tough woman who could handle herself well, and he was not the biggest guy. I was worried that he might dump her and leave her with no resources.

She had a family in North Carolina, and the problem was that she was so embarrassed by the fact that she had left North Carolina and her parents. Her family told her not to do it. They did not trust him, and they were adamant that this was not a good idea, so she left quickly to be with him. This made it difficult for her to go back and say, "Hey, I screwed up. Please let me come back to North Carolina."

I encouraged her to do that and then tried to explain to her that everybody makes mistakes, we all do dumb things sometimes, and that's it.

Regardless, because she had withdrawn her petition, he was no longer eligible for any immigration benefits, and his application was denied.

Chicago Birth Certificates

I had a case out of Chicago. I had a gentleman from West Africa come into my office. He had married an African-American woman.

This couple did not appear to be a good match. This is one of the cases involving an obese woman. Additionally, she was not well-kept and not aesthetically attractive. One of the beauties of life is the old saying, *Love is blind,* but it is not true. Granted, some couples have mismatched weight, looks, or whatever, and that's wonderful; however, in life, the exception is not the rule, and for immigration, that is the case as well.

Many single scheme, one-sided fraud scams exist where U.S. citizens are preyed upon by attractive and well-spoken foreigners looking to exploit the system. In this case, the USC lady was humble and not a mean person. You could tell that she had low self-esteem from talking to her and getting her story. I interviewed her and the immigrant spouse regarding the marriage.

What I recall out of this case was that she had some serious issues with the marriage. Surprisingly, she doubted the marriage herself. She did get into the marriage for the right reasons. She wanted to marry him. But he was often neglectful and did not come home for days. He treated her as a roommate and not a spouse. He did not want to share a bed with her. He could be verbally abusive. You could tell she was hurt by it. But she made it clear that she desperately wanted to be married and wanted to be loved; that's what she was hoping for. Those were her words to me. You see, sometimes the (ninety-day visas for fiancés?) relationships are tragic.

In this case, the gentleman I was interviewing had a bad law enforcement record. I looked him up in the database and found he had a completely different name and a different social security number. He had a different identity than the one he was portraying, and his American wife herself brought in documents to show. They had been married for a brief time, less than two years, and the American wife's suspicions grew over time. She did her investigation due to growing concerns, wisely snooped around, and found documents questioning the identity of her immigrant husband.

This was the case as I looked through her stuff and through database information. He bought a house under a fraudulent name and Social Security number. And they were living in the house that he had bought under the assumed name.

So, I had to do an investigation on this. I found an interesting years-old case, one of the thousands of cases where immigrants masked their identity. I reached out to the investigators in Chicago, where this fraud case was originally. I found this immigrant was part of a group in cahoots with some women, legal U.S. citizens living in Chicago. These women were going to vital records and getting birth certificates for children. The woman claimed the children were born at home. They would then sell these birth certificates to immigrants who paid them for the certificates. The immigrants would order a Social Security number for that child. They would then wash out the date of birth and use the birth certificate and the Social Security card to get jobs, open bank accounts, and get home on loans. These were legitimate birth certificates issued by the state and sold to individuals to create fake identities.

Similarly, we had a case in a Texas and California midwives case where parents of children born in Mexico would have midwives claim the child was born in Texas or California to obtain real citizenship documents under false statements. That is another story.

In the end, he was denied based on the false claim to U.S. citizenship. Any time you use documents to claim citizenship and you are not a citizen, then that is a problem. He had obtained a HUD home loan by doing this.

I do not know how this affected the U.S. citizen. I imagine she was both devastated and perhaps glad that she at least got to the truth.

Fake Dead Wife

U.S. Citizenship and Immigration Services (USCIS) receives thousands of tip letters a year. But this was an interesting one from a father-in-law. A Nigerian man came to this country to visit. Oftentimes, when people are coming into this country, they will look for a sponsor that ensures a place to stay or to look after them while here. In this case, the visitor asked his father-in-law, who is also Nigerian, to write a letter sponsoring him. His father-in-law emigrated years ago. The visiting Nigerian man asked his father-in-law to write him a letter of recommendation to visit. It's not uncommon for people to write a letter to the Department of State saying, "Hey, I know John Smith or whoever, and I'd like him to come over." The letter will go on to say something like, "I'm responsible for him, I'll make sure he has a place to stay, etc."

The interesting thing is, the way the U.S. Department of State works, they might not let the actual family member come over, out of concern family members will not leave upon expiration of the visit or vacation. The State Department said they would let his son-in-law come to the U.S. The State Department wouldn't let the man's daughter and son-in-law come together for fear that a married couple would get over here and they would stay.

The son-in-law gets here and doesn't stay with his father-in-law. The son-in-law had some friends over here that the father-in-law didn't know about. His now son-in-law found another woman to marry, a U.S. citizen, an African-American female. The son-in-law has his new bride, a U.S. citizen, file the I-130 visa petition for him. Additionally, the new couple filed an I-485 (application to register permanent residence or adjust status) at the same time, a common occurrence, right?

In the filing process, this Nigerian man (son-in-law) submits a death certificate for his former Nigerian wife. The death certificate shows that she was in a motorcycle accident and tragically hit by a car. Subsequently, he wrote a letter saying, "My previous wife died in Nigeria. So, I didn't go home, and I met the love of my life in the U.S." Now, this was quick; you got to remember he came over here through his father-in-law, his wife suddenly died in Nigeria, and quickly he married a USC female. A tragic and amazing turn of events.

Somehow, the father-in-law got wind of this, quite surprised that his daughter had died. Fortunately for the father-in-law, we have great phones now, and his daughter explained to him in a phone call that she was very much alive!

There was some speculation that the daughter may have been informed of the husband's plot: "Sit tight once I get my benefits and everything, I'll divorce my African American wife and marry you again (my true love from home), and you'll get the immigration benefits as well." This is not as uncommon as you might think. I have had a few foreign spouses come back to life.

I don't think she was up for that plan because she said, "How will I come back from the dead? Since the motorcycle accident killed me. I can't come back alive; no one will believe my resurrection."

The father-in-law wasn't happy about his son-in-law's manipulation of his daughter and the immigration system and wrote a letter to U.S. immigration officers in evidence that his daughter was still alive. Now, this is a challenging thing, right? You have a death certificate saying that his Nigerian wife is dead. I have two people saying that she's still alive. There's no substantive proof on the side that she's still alive; the official document from Nigeria says she's dead. As U.S. immigration officers, we have to be careful that the reverse is not happening. Somebody could be playing a game with us to try to get the son-in-law in trouble. And all we have is letters from the father-in-law and daughter, with no identification or anything. This goes on for a few months, and we can't find the son-in-law to talk to him and see what's going on.

Eventually, the daughter, or supposed deceased first wife, comes into the country from Nigeria. U.S. Immigration sets up an interview with her, and she comes in to see me. She has identifying documents: a passport from Nigeria, a birth certificate, and a government ID. She gives her testimony and explains what's going on. At this point, we thought we had sufficient evidence that the husband/son-in-law was committing fraud. This is kind of a hilarious immigration fraud that happens.

As a side story, I had a colleague from an African country, he was also an immigration officer. His country had gone through a civil war at one time. He had an interview with a man who said his wife had been raped and murdered. The husband was an eyewitness to the crime. A bit of investigation showed his wife was actually alive and well. The officer shows him evidence that his wife in that country was still alive, and the guy didn't miss a beat. He jumped up, slapped himself on the head, and said, "Oh my God. My wife is still alive, thank you, thank you! I'm so happy now."

He was sitting there with his USC wife. He had planned to sneak his wife in at a later date and ride on his refugee status, so we suspected that he knew that his real wife was already still alive.

These examples are not as rare as you may think. I have had many cases where a spouse in a foreign country has died. Car accidents, murders, heart attacks—whatever. But miraculously, they come back alive or even come back with completely different names and dates of birth. Now, the Department of State fingerprints applicants. It is a bit harder, but people still try.

After the Border

Marriage Fraud Rings

The third marriage fraud that you see is arranged marriages. In these arranged marriages, you have a broker, whom I'll call an arranger. It's usually an immigrant who may or may not have citizenship. The arrangers have deep ties to their foreign communities. The larger kingpin arrangers have a pool of henchmen called handlers, who walk the engaged couples through the courthouse process. The arrangers also have good ties to the local communities in the United States, completing the pipeline. Most of the arrangers were men, but some were women. Many were foreigners. But there were also many U.S. Citizens who ran these enterprises. Kind of different from the musical *Fiddler on the Roof,* where the young women would sing to an elderly woman, "Matchmaker, matchmaker, make me a match," swooning for a husband. Unfortunately, it's not like the romantic musical—this is fraud on a large scale, designed to flood the system and America with immigrants.

Often, the arranger is or was married to a U.S. citizen through someone else's fraud ring. The arranger has firsthand knowledge of the process, sometimes with the assistance of his ex-wife, who was born in America. They got married. She helped him get his green card and his legal permanent resident status. They're now divorced. The arranger is back with his real wife from his home country; however, they both live in America after playing the system like a violin. His U.S. citizen ex-wife has gone on to other relationships. But the arranger and his American ex-wife maintain a lucrative marriage-fraud business arrangement.

The arranger, who's either a citizen or permanent resident (green card), brings in other immigrants. The U.S. wife or ex-wife often becomes a recruiter of other U.S. citizens to marry immigrants. U.S. citizens recruited to marry immigrants into our country usually make 500 bucks off the fake marriage. After the money is paid and the deal is done, the arranger will say, "Hey, I think I can make you more money; bring some more people in to marry." It's the same thing that you see in an apartment complex referral; bring in a new tenant, and we'll give you a free month's rent. Immigration fraud networks work the same way.

Immigration fraud, immigration, and immigration employment are all big money makers. We're talking about anywhere from US$6,000 to US$10,000 per marriage. That's what the immigrants pay. Back at the southern border, the cartels charge about the same fee to get you across the border into the U.S. The U.S. citizen faking being the loving spouse gets between $500 and $2,000 per marriage.

Some immigrants who can't pay the whole tab become indentured servants to the arrangers. For example, an immigrant needs to pay a $10,000 fee to the marriage arranger, and usually, they don't have that money upfront. They must pay it off over time. Kingpin financing is no picnic. Immigrants will be thrust into joining the arranger in committing higher-level financial fraud, regardless of whether they're good people or not. They're trapped in illegal marriage fraud, plus working two or three jobs or worse, joining in financial fraud to pay that $10,000 off the debt. I've had grown men from West Africa bawling their eyes out in my office. The immigrant would tell me, "I have to pay the U.S. citizen to stay married to me. That's one job. I have to pay the arranger to set up the marriage and help me through the process; that's another job. Then I have to live and pay for myself (my third job). And I have to pay for the real family I have from my home country or also living in America (a fourth job)." This is the unfortunate story I've heard often.

I told this gentleman who was a banker, and he was pro-immigrant. He looked at me, and he said, "You know, that's hyperbole. None of that happens." He didn't believe it.

The other thing about fraud that I want you to know about is, there's so much fraud and so much conversation about fraud that it's difficult to keep track of it all. What is the other danger of this systemic level of marriage fraud? It gets drowned out. The problem is most people see it as not that big of a deal. I was stunned to hear that response from the banker.

Many people involved in marriage fraud are involved in all kinds of other fraud. That's one of their stepping stones to larger crime. An immigrant needs that green card, then citizenship, to get into the bigger rackets beyond marriage fraud. Like Financial fraud.

Most often, they get in here, they do marriage fraud, analogous to a gateway drug, and then they're hooked in the crime world, moving up to a higher schedule of financial fraud. Most of the time, when I was investigating a marriage fraud case, I was on the phone with some other law enforcement officer or agent who was piling up more charges against the immigrant who originally committed marriage fraud. One case attached to the person that I was investigating included financial fraud, social security fraud, FEMA fraud, Walmart game card fraud, and identity theft. I think 80 percent of my cases encompassed one of those forms of fraud.

I want you to understand that I use the word *fraud* far more loosely than the U.S. Immigration Service uses fraud. Fraud as defined by U.S. Immigration, is a person convicted of fraud. Meaning they took them through the court system and tried them. That's almost impossible, especially in Atlanta. In the twenty years I was in the Atlanta office, we prosecuted two marriage fraud rings. Of the more than 2,000 marriage fraud cases that I worked on, only one percent were charged. We were able to prove there were marriage fraud rings with a significant number of people involved, but none were ever prosecuted because one specific Assistant U.S. attorney would not prosecute. All cases were funneled through him, and U.S. Immigration could only conclude that Atlanta did not and would not prosecute immigration fraud. This Assistant U.S. attorney of Atlanta did everything he could to not prosecute and to make sure that these cases were never prosecuted by sitting on the cases. So, you could never technically say *fraud* for most marriage fraud cases.

If you could get the immigrant in deportation proceedings and take your evidence before an immigration judge by issuing a notice to appear, you could have an immigration judge find them in marriage fraud; however, none of these cases met the priority for going before an immigration judge. Because the immigrant had not committed or been convicted of another crime. So, they were not going before an immigration judge, resulting in a finding of marriage fraud. It never happened in the twenty years that I was in Atlanta.

The third way is that you could have a marriage fraud conviction if you had an admission of marriage fraud. You have a better chance of finding a needle in a haystack than getting an immigrant to admit to marriage fraud. U.S. citizens? Yes, U.S. citizens would confess all the time. You need detailed proof of the fraud. It is not enough for a U.S. citizen to admit to being married fraudulently. They must give specific details beyond basic testimony.

Officers go out into the field and find all this evidence that the couple never was in a real marriage. Did they use fake documents to prove their marriage? Fake leases? Fake tax records? Fraudulent insurance records, doctored photos, and even written and audio confessions?

The courts have tough criteria for immigration officers to determine fraud. Also, the courts have their own biases and leanings. So we write it up often as fraud, and we would make an assessment of fraud, but in reality, it does not meet the legal definition of the finding of fraud because we cannot get the case before a court. It is not what you know; it is what you can prove. And with the DOJ suspiciously not wanting to prosecute, it's about a one in a thousand chance of getting a conviction. Let's look at some of the Counties and other cities these cases.

All in the Family

This story is one of my first fraud cases that involved more than two people. The Atlanta office had shifted, and we'd been working out of the downtown office (a beautiful building called the Old Post Office, architecture from the 1930s). I loved the building, but it was falling apart. When it rained, water ran down inside the walls. So, they moved us up to the Ashford Dunwoody Offices (North of Atlanta) for a while. We worked out of an office with everyone assigned to cubicles, which made it difficult to complete private interviews. I was working on one application when an African-American gentleman came in with his African wife. The couple seemed a bit odd, and the African-American male did not appear to know much about his African bride. After asking for more information from the couple about their marriage, I finished the interview and set the file aside for more documents (bills, leases, etc.).

Lo and behold, the same gentleman came back the next day with a completely different Nigerian wife, and that raised suspicions, to say the least! He was in the office twice in two days with two different foreign wives. I did more research about his filing and found that he had filed for six Nigerian women to adjust their immigration status, and all those cases were pending. He had married all the foreign women in Gwinnett County, Georgia. All these marriages took place in less than six months.

Upon further research, I found an African-American woman had also married six Nigerian men. Again, but in reverse, all six of the African men had married one African-American woman! During my investigation, between these six women and these six men, there was a further Nigerian connection: they were all husbands and wives from Africa, six Nigerian married couples in their homeland. Even more interesting, the U.S. citizen African American woman who married the six Nigerian men and the U.S. citizen African American man who married the six Nigerian women were related.

All twelve filings were bundled and sent to Fraud Detection and National Security (FDNS). FDNS reached out to Homeland Security Investigations (HSI), which completes criminal investigations.

This isn't a one-day investigation to get everything done; it generally takes several months between sending it all off to the agencies and completing their investigative work.

As I suspected, the case was eventually declined by prosecutors in both HSI and the United States Attorney's office. FDNS sent the files back to me. The case was not large enough and not "sexy enough" for prosecution. This was conveyed to me on a Monday.

I was fuming and furious about the whole process. I'm like, come on, you don't prosecute, and you've got this really interesting case. Justice should be able to get something out of it, so I went home on Monday a little bit mad about it. Before I left, I bundled the files up and prepared the files to be sent to the records center and shipped them out of the office.

The next morning, I was driving into town listening to the radio, and I heard the most infuriating thing you could ever imagine. It was someone going on about Alvin Lorenzo Murdock, who had been arrested by Gwinnett County Sheriff's offices for polygamy. And I'm like, that's my Alvin Murdock, that's my guy! Gwinnett County arrested him, and it wasn't more than a few seconds after I got into the office that one of my colleagues who had interviewed Murdoch and one of the other women came to me. They had also heard them on the radio about Murdoch's arrest. My phone started ringing off the hook. Because the media had gotten involved, FDNS and HSI were interested.

"A Gwinnett County, Georgia man facing bigamy charges was behind bars Thursday. A court clerk tipped off police after noticing thirty-eight-year-old Alvin Lorenzo Murdock had applied for several marriage licenses.

"Police arrested Murdock Monday, and they said he was trying to help women stay in the U.S. So far, the investigation shows that Mr. Murdock has married approximately six different women in the past five months. We believe his intent was to help them become U.S. citizens, said Officer Darren Maloney of the Gwinnett County Police.

"If convicted, Murdock could face a five-year prison sentence for each count against him, and police said he may also face federal charges."

It is difficult to get the Atlanta U.S. attorney's office to take any immigration cases, especially marriage fraud cases.

In my twenty years with the service, we prosecuted two marriage fraud rings—that's it. Now granted, one of those probably saw twenty arrangers convicted over a number of years. It is often a long process and involves multiple people who either arrange or recruit others to enter marriages. But that is a drop in the bucket.

In the article, the local sheriff's department officer who mentioned possible federal prosecution would most likely be shocked by our apathy. At least the Gwinnett County sheriff had arrested the man for polygamy.

The African American female wanted in connection to marriage to the six African men was Shawnta McBride. I never heard if she was found or arrested by Gwinnett County.

I did not hear any more about this case for close to seven years. By that time, I was a fraud detection officer. One of the cases had come back to FDNS. The six women who married Murdock had all filed I-360: Petition for Amerasian, Widow(er), or Special Immigrant under the Violence Against Women Act (VAWA). Specifically, they filed as battered spouses. In their claim, they stated they knew nothing about each other's marriage to Murdoch. The service center in the state of Vermont handles all these cases. Vermont granted their petitions, so they could then become permanent residence. I do not believe the men were granted the same benefits, nor any of the others involved in the fraud. Just those women.

By marrying all of them, Vermont Service Center facilitated and allowed polygamous marriages. They all knew what was going on, but Vermont Center granted those things in a second, and all ended up being approved.

Just like the next story, if you think things work out, they don't.

Walhalla, South Carolina, Marriages from the Norse Gods

This is a birth certificate story, a case of fraudulent marriages out of Walhalla, South Carolina, and also spelled Valhalla in Viking mythology. Viking warriors' Valhalla is known as a magical place where the souls of war heroes enjoy a heavenly afterlife. Some marriages are magical and heavenly. Not this one.

Walhalla, South Carolina, is a small town with 4,000 residents, give or take a few hundred. You would not foresee a small town as a hotbed of immigrant Indian and Pakistani men marrying African-American women. At least not in the numbers that Immigration tracked spiking upward in this small town. Especially since none of the Indians, Pakistanis, or African Americans lived in Walhalla, maybe Viking mysticism drew them to this sleepy small town.

The way this fraud ring worked: foreign males entered the U.S. on visitor visas. They were living in New York City and the surrounding northeast region of the country. These guys somehow managed to meet women from Atlanta and drive 120 miles to Walhalla, South Carolina, to get married.

These Indian and Pakistani men would come down from New York to the Atlanta, Georgia area and meet with African-American women. After the meeting, they would drive up to Walhalla, South Carolina to get married. We saw quite a few of these cases going on in this small town.

One day, this young Indian male in his mid-twenties and his African-American wife came to my office for an interview. The African-American woman had filed an I-130 visa petition for the Indian man as her husband.

I interviewed them based on the claimed marriage. Typically, in the Walhalla cases, the husband and wife had known each other a short time before marrying.

I generally ask questions about how, when, and where they met and how long the relationship had been going on. When you interview, you need to ask sufficient questions to see if they know each other. New questions often flow from the prior question.

You are trying to piece a puzzle together. You need the applicants' help in creating the image of the relationship. Sometimes, that puzzle is missing some key pieces. Sometimes, the pieces do not fit. This is when we really start to question the relationship if they can't help us form the puzzle picture. If they cannot fill in the blanks to solve the larger puzzle, then you get a sense this marriage is not good. Often, when it's a fraudulent marriage, they will pick dates they claimed to meet that are easy to remember, especially when they don't know anything about each other. They may barely know each other's names. In some cases, they don't even know that. So, they try to tell their stories around dates that are significant, like holidays.

During the interview, this is the story the Walhalla newlyweds gave me: They met on February 14, 2004, Valentine's Day. The two of them dated for two weeks and then got married around the first of March. During the interview, they also presented a birth certificate for their claimed child. The child was born on May 1, 2004.

Due to these facts, I had to be detailed and often asked questions more than once. I asked several times when they first met. They always claimed February 14, 2004. I had to ask, "Is there any chance you could have met earlier? Say August or September of the prior year?"

They were adamant that they had never met before February 14. Mind you, the child's father on the birth certificate was this young Indian male. My next question is, "Was there any complication during the pregnancy? Was their child born early or carried to full term?"

The girl stated, "There were no complications, and the child was carried to full term."

I expressed to the couple that I was not sure the Indian male could be the father if they met in February, married in March, and the young lady had a child the first week of May. Do the math. I told them at best, the gestation period was only three months. And the child couldn't have been carried to full term. Perhaps Walhalla/Valhalla did have magical powers!

At one time, U.S. Immigration was allowed to ask for a DNA test. That is not the case today. So, at the time, I requested a DNA test for the child. The test results took a few weeks to come back, and then I got a knock on my office door from the newlywed Indian husband.

He looked downtrodden. He presented the envelope with the results. The Results clearly showed 99.9 percent that he was *not* the father. I was kind of shocked they even went through the process. There was no way he was the father, and she at least knew it, even if he did not. They were praying to the Walhalla Viking baby fairy for better results, and the young Indian man didn't meet the warrior muster to inherit the magic of Valhalla/Walhalla, South Carolina.

I denied the case based on the DNA test and falsified interview. All the evidence showed the marriage was not bonafide for immigration purposes, but not to the standard of criminal fraud. Maybe Walhalla gave them some good fortune.

Georgia Revenue Girl, Part 1

This is a two-part story: Georgia Revenue Girl and Belletrist. The first story, Georgia Revenue Girl, involves multiple people. This story is not isolated. This is a common theme that I dealt with as an immigration officer. I dealt with the types of twists and turns in this story daily. The falsehoods. The doublespeak. The twisted logic was constant.

I hope, as a reader, you are not overly confused. But I want you to be confused to some degree because I was confused or pushed to the limit from dealing with the labyrinth of fraud and homegrown ideological forces working against me and the United States for most of my career.

Where to begin? From the middle, it's probably the best I can do since I got this case in the middle of its duration.

One of the U.S. Immigration Service officers had already interviewed him. During the interview process, officers had some questions. There was some chaos or confusion related to this applicant. The story and case are loosely linked to a G-2 visa case. G-2 visas are other representatives of a designated international organization. In this case, the G-2 visa holders were coming to attend meetings in the United States. When it comes to immigration, many of these different avenues are intertwined and interconnected in multiple ways.

If you look at the history of immigration, it's groups of people from specific countries going to the same spot, connecting, and creating communities. Nigerians, Indians, Ghanaians, Chinese, Russians, Polish, Swedish, Italians … It doesn't matter. They've all done the same thing. They come in, they find a place where they feel safe and comfortable, and that's where they lay down their roots. It's the history of immigration. Therefore, within those communities, they work out systems. They have connectivity. They get married to someone they met two days ago or three weeks ago. That's arranged, that's prepared. It's common. It happens a hundred times a day. Every day in Atlanta. It happens all over the country continuously, constantly. The Nigerians whom I've dealt with have networks throughout the entire country. Most of my fraud schemes were interconnected to the major cities, such as Philadelphia, Oakland, Houston, Boston, New York City, Chicago, and Atlanta … all highly connected or organized systems for marriage fraud and financial fraud. It is not a small-scale thing.

This story called *Georgia Revenue Girl* is no different.

First, I set up a site visit. We call it a bed check or home check. We went to this house from the case file address. I always try to get to a location at 6:00 in the morning. Generally, I want to be at the house a little earlier than that. You may ask, why? Why do you want to be there at 6:00 in the morning again?

People go to work, right? So, I must be there before they go to work. The nice thing about getting there early is you can scope out the neighborhood. You can see what's coming and going, who's up, who's not up. Who's leaving early, and who's not? I usually sit in front of the house or near the house to watch and see if the lights come on.

When you see lights come on, you know people are up and getting ready to go do something. I would often sit there for fifteen or twenty minutes after the lights came on. Give them a minute to do whatever: brush their teeth or go to the bathroom. That was usually my rule. I'm a guest in their house. They can refuse me entry into their home.

Regardless, we go to their home and wait for the lights to come on. I knock on the door. The sun's up, its summertime, around 7 a.m. It's light out. In this case, at this home, a woman comes to the door. And this woman is Nigerian. I'm here to see a male Nigerian immigrant. I asked this young lady who she was, and she told me her name. Let's call her Belletrist to maintain confidentiality. Belletrist had come into the country on an F-1 student visa (full-time academic student at an accredited university).

A gentleman was standing behind her, a large guy, 6' 4" or 6' 5", 250 pounds. The exact description of the person I was looking for.

I asked him his name; he gave me a completely different name. I asked him for his identification and he said he didn't have any. I asked them both, Belletrist and the big guy, if the gentleman I was looking for was home. I explained to the big guy that he looked similar to the person that I was looking for. I said, "You match him pretty darn close, and your photo looks exactly like him. He shrugged and said, "I'm not him, I'm his cousin."

I talked to Belletrist to get a little more information. I took a photo of her passport photo and visa. She allowed me to do that. I thanked them, and I left.

Two days later, we did another site visit, this time for the big guy's American spouse. A tax lady who worked for the Georgia Department of Revenue had petitioned for her immigrant spouse, known to us as the big guy. In our records, everything checked out that she lived in an apartment in DeKalb County, Georgia.

The same scenario: I got there early. Wait for the lights to come on. Wait for something to happen. In this instance, it was kind of difficult because she lived in an apartment on the second floor. There weren't a lot of windows in it. It's always difficult, but I couldn't see if she was there, so we waited until about 7:00 a.m. Then I knocked on the door. I knocked several times. There was no answer. When people don't answer the door, I will call them. I called her phone a couple of times. There was no answer. We checked the parking lot and found her car. We still couldn't tell if she was there or not.

At about 7:30 in the morning, we decided to leave. The tax lady was not answering the door. She's not answering her phone. She's not going to come to the door.

The tax lady worked for the Georgia Department of Revenue. The U.S. citizen petitioning for the immigrant big guy was doing your taxes. This is from a government official responsible for reviewing your tax records.

Since there was no answer at the tax lady's apartment, I decided to go to her office and talk to her there. Accompanied by a Homeland Security

Investigations agent, we went up to the Georgia Department of Revenue in the Atlanta area. I speak to the director of the Department of Revenue there. She's a nice lady. I think she retired from the federal government and was now working for the state of Georgia. She agreed to allow me to speak to the young lady that I was looking for. We hung out in a conference room while they went to get her.

Our USC spouse is immediately a little perturbed. I don't blame her. I'm at her office, talking to her coworkers. But my thinking is, *all you had to do is open your apartment door*. She had a reasonable excuse for why she didn't open her door that day. She was in the shower. I didn't know that. She could have called me back and left me a message. But she didn't do any of that, so I came to her office. The tax lady told me she had an attorney and that she didn't want to talk to me without her attorney present.

I thanked her, and we left, nothing to it.

Interestingly, the unwritten motto of government tax revenue collectors is, if we must come to you, you're in deep trouble. Kind of like, don't let me get out of this chair, which you'd hear from an adult when you were a kid misbehaving. If you don't file your taxes, avoid the collection or appearance notices by tax collectors, then they send an agent out to you. In this case, U.S. Immigration was tracking down the tax lady because she avoided us at her apartment and didn't return my calls, which was maybe a "practice what you preach" moment.

Since the tax lady's Nigerian immigrant spouse, the big guy told me he was not the person I was looking for, another twist to the story emerged. As with the tax lady, I went to the big guy's place of employment, or what I thought was his place of work. U.S. Immigration could check on things and look people up in a multitude of ways. As an immigration officer, one of the things we can do is we can run your Social Security number through any number of systems, and we can find out a lot of information about you. In my process of looking at the big guy, I found that he was working at a small company in the Atlanta area.

It was a small, corrugated building. A shop-type thing. They were building small machinery or something. I didn't pay a lot of attention to that. I wasn't there to assess the company.

So, I went up and asked the people who ran the business. I showed my credentials to the shop owner and explained what I was there for. You never tell them you're doing an investigation, and you don't tip anything off to the employer. You say, "Hey, I'd like to talk to your employee, the big guy. He's got some benefits that he's applying for."

All true. And we're verifying information about the big guy. Everything from our standpoint as U.S. immigration officers that we are telling the shop owner is true. There's no reason to lie.

I asked the shop owner if they knew the big guy by name. They said yes, the big guy does work there. He's been working there for some time, and the big guy is here on shift.

They usher us into a conference room to have a seat, and we wait. Employers would always be concerned. They always think there's something terrible going on. You must relieve the fears of that and make them feel a little better about what's going on.

This is where I should remind you the big guy is big; I'm looking for a 6'4" or 6'5" 260-pound man. They bring in the big guy, who's probably 5'4" and I'm guessing, 120 pounds.

I do a double-take on him. Because I'm like, *I know whom I'm looking for. This is not him.* But I play along. I started asking him questions about his marriage and where he lives. Now, I start asking about his wife. I can see that he is really confused.

Little Fella says, "I applied for immigration benefits years ago in Florida, and I was denied. And my wife and I got divorced years ago, and we're not married anymore."

I look at him and go, "You're not the big guy," and give the name of the big guy.

The Little Fella answers, "No, I'm not."

I said to Little Fella, "Well, how did you get the big guy's name? How did you get the big guy's Social Security number to start using it to get a job and to work?"

And he explained to me that he knew the big guy and met him through someone, and Little Fella paid the big guy money to use his name and

Social Security number to get a job. So the big guy, not even with a green card yet, the person I'm looking for, had already sold his Social Security number and identity!

This led me to a larger investigation into the big guy. Was the big guy the kingpin of a big fraud network? Had the tax lady, with a good-paying career and benefits, been swept into a fraud ring? I'm looking forward to the process of doing my investigation, digging deep, and speaking to more people in the potential fraud network. What I found out is the big guy, who's not even a legal permanent resident, is aiding and assisting other people in getting benefits through the U.S. immigration process. The big guy arranges marriages for people and helps them get Social Security cards. He's helping immigrants get different fraudulent benefits through the federal government. I ended up finding out the big guy assisted more than fifteen people, and he hasn't even gotten his immigration benefits straightened out yet. Welcome to America. You can't make this stuff up, it's so brazen and crazy!

This leads me to go through his file more thoroughly. I go to different places where the big guy has claimed to live. Also, I checked on the tax lady, the big guy's U.S. citizen petitioner for marriage and residency. I found out that a lot of the documents that they've submitted, their lease agreements, they're checking account information, bills ... everything all fraudulent. It's all bogus.

I talked to the landlords. Showed the lease agreements. The landlord confirmed the submitted lease forms were altered and not valid.

I go through the extended network part of the big guy's scam, and I've bundled up seven or eight different files of immigrants in the big guy's fraud network that he's helped. I couldn't get the best evidence of the remaining immigrants caught up in the fraud, but I got enough evidence to get the skinny on what he was doing.

I called **everyone** into the immigration office. Each of the applicants admitted he had arranged their marriages.

I sent the big guy a letter, and I sent his attorney a letter, too. The tax lady and the big guy as a couple and their attorney showed up at the office.

This is not a long interview. I've got a ton of information on them. I started interviewing them, and I started with the U.S. citizen, the tax lady. Again, she is irate. The tax lady is a little hostile. She doesn't appreciate the fact that I made her come to the immigration office. I reminded the tax lady that the interview was strictly voluntary and that she could leave or end the interview at any time.

I always start by inviting the interviewee to tell their story. I let them answer questions in a way they feel most comfortable related to the story that they want to tell. Most of the interviews that I do are fraudulent, so they're going to tell false stories. That's why I'm there. I'm not there for any other reason than eliciting information. I've done the research, or I've gotten testimony that shows a fraudulent marriage. Nine times out of ten, I know it is a fraudulent marriage. But it is not what you know; it is what you can prove.

I let them tell their story, how they met, and where they lived: as much about the relationship that they can come up with or they've concocted. I ask the big guy questions on their leases and the other documents that they've submitted, whether it's their taxes, lease agreements, bills, phone bills, whatever they've submitted to U.S. Immigration to prove either their identity or that they're married to each other. You want them to be able to sit there and tell you their marriage story.

Frankly, if you've submitted to me a fraudulent lease agreement, and I tell you it's a fraudulent lease agreement, you're going to clam up. It's going to be hard for me to use it against you. Instead, I like to ask, "Is this your lease agreement from 87 Mockingbird Lane?"

And then usually they'll say yes.

"Did you sign this lease agreement together?"

"Yes."

You may ask about the apartment or home. You let them answer on their terms without telling them whether it seems fraudulent or whether you have different evidence from the landlord. You have to remember these individuals are under oath, and if they give contradictory statements to the facts and evidence, then they are now held accountable for the story, and you could theoretically prosecute them for that alone. Most people will stick to their stories and will tell you that's their signature.

"How did you meet? Where did you meet? Where do you live? What's going on in your life?" But I hadn't gotten to any of the documents yet.

In this case, when I got to the part of the interview to ask questions about the documents, the tax lady already knew the jig was up. I started on the documents and presented her with a lease agreement. I knew the lease agreement was fraudulent, so I said, "Hey, is this your lease agreement for 1919 Mockingbird Lane?"

The tax lady's answer was, "I don't understand the question."

So then I asked her, "OK, looking at this lease," as I showed her the lease and put it in front of her face. I said, "Is this your name on the top of this lease agreement?"

And she answered me, "I do not understand the question." The tax lady was smug.

Then I flipped the page to the last page of the lease agreement, and I said, "Hey, is this your signature on this lease agreement for 1919 Mockingbird Lane?"

She said, "I do not understand the question."

I tried several different ways to get her to answer the question. The attorney finally jumped in and said, "Officer, she clearly doesn't understand any of your questions."

I go to the next document. It's the same thing.

I go to the next question, and the same thing: "I do not understand your question. I do not understand what you're asking. I do not understand."

That's all she would say to me from then on. I typed all of this up with each of the questions that I asked her. The U.S. citizen tax lady answered every question the same way, "I don't understand the question."

I knew this wasn't going to go anywhere. I laid everything out in front of the tax lady. I knew in all the cases in the big guy's fraud network that the tax lady was aiding and abetting other immigrants to try to get benefits. All of the documents that I did the legwork for turned out to be fraudulent. As you remember, the little guy was working at the machine shop.

I asked the big guy if he was the man at the door when I came to his residence, and he didn't want to admit it. He said that was his cousin, even though it was the same guy sitting in my office.

This had gotten so ridiculous that their attorney asked to speak to his two clients alone. You always allow them to do that. Maybe you're going to get a confession. Maybe they're going to withdraw, maybe something like that. Maybe he will drop his clients as an attorney. Any of that stuff can happen. Attorneys will indicate they don't want to represent them anymore.

In this case, he spoke to the big guy and tax lady for a few minutes. The attorney came back to me. He states, "As an attorney, I can't allow my clients to continue with this interview. There's, you know, derogatory information that you have. I think we should cease this interview today." There was nothing I could do. It's a voluntary interview. They decided to leave, and so they left the interview. And that's the end of it.

I'm not an adjudicator. I don't get to approve or deny the case. I wrote it up and explained what was going on. I sent it to Homeland Security Investigations to see if they wanted to take this case, including the other activities that Big Guy was involved in. And, of course, as usual, they declined. It wasn't "sexy enough" or large enough. You know, I thought they would take it for the fact that the tax lady was a state employee working for the Georgia Department of Revenue which scares me still to this day. If she commits major immigration fraud, then what will she do to your taxes?

For me, I thought this was the end of the case. The case got kicked back to our service, the USCIS (U.S. Citizenship and Immigration Services). USCIS would approve or deny the application and petition, and that would be the end of it. He would be put in proceedings for removal or be granted legal permanent residence.

This was not the case. I think five months passed. I got an email from headquarters related to the big guy who had been in the United States for probably five or six years. I knew that he had a real Nigerian wife in the United States, and they had kids here, too.

U.S. Immigration was being contacted by Canadian Immigration. The big guy had been doing fraud in the U.S. and was scared that he was not simply going to get deported but prosecuted and convicted in the U.S. So the big guy decided to flee the United States and go to Canada.

When he went to Canada, he changed his name again. This could have been his real name for all I know, but it was a completely different name. When he got to Canada, the big guy applied for asylum in Canada. The big guy applied with his wife and children, not with the tax lady, his U.S. citizen wife, but with his actual wife and children. I have no idea what Canada did with this. I think Canadians have a basic asylum process, the same as most of the world does. Generally, you don't give someone asylum if they're coming from a third country and immigrated to a first-world country where they're already safe. In other words, he might have come from Nigeria and been in danger, but the fact that he was living in the United States for five years means he wasn't eligible for asylum in Canada. He would have had to file for asylum in the United States under his original name. It turned out the big guy could tell some big lies.

This leads me to the second story of Belletrist, whom we first met when the big guy stood behind her at the apartment. Belletrist was in the U.S. on an F-1 student visa (full-time academic student at an accredited university).

Belletrist Georgia Revenue Girl, Part 2

We first met Belletrist when the big guy stood behind her in the previous story. This one is a continuation with a focus on Belletrist's case. All we knew was that Belletrist was a student standing at the door with the big guy, an immigrant fraud ringleader who eventually had to flee the country to Canada for fear of prosecution in the U.S. What of Belletrist? How would she fare being associated with a cunning and brazen scammer?

I took photos of Belletrist's visa and ID. When I got back to the U.S. Immigration Office, I ran her, kind of like a patrol cop runs someone's license plates, but with more databases. Belletrist did live in the big guy's home, which is a requirement for immigration officers; anyone who lives in the home of an applicant should be run and checked to make sure there are no issues like a criminal record. Belletrist's visa showed she came to the U.S. as an F-1 student; however, she wasn't going to school anywhere, which nowadays is common. Many F-1 students come into the country and never go to school.

I ran my background checks on Belletrist, and then I did what is called a lookout on this young lady's case. I put her name and pertinent information in a system that other law enforcement and DHS agency personnel could access. If anyone encountered her, when they ran checks, her name would pop up. After she came in, my prediction was within a certain period, Belletrist would find a U.S. citizen to marry. My hunch was correct: about one year after my investigation of the big guy's case, Belletrist filed for legal residence after marrying a much older gentleman. I looked for the old guy, but I couldn't find him. My experience said he was homeless ... I never saw him and couldn't find him anywhere. Why? It's almost impossible to track down homeless people.

Paperwork was filed for Belletrist to become a legal permanent resident. She went through an interview process. I had a lookout, suspecting that she would be appearing through the database to facilitate her immigrant status via marriage to a U.S. citizen. Sure enough, after her first interview, the immigration service officer sent the file to me. I reviewed Belletrist's information, and she claimed to live in the same house I'd gone to before.

I went back to the house once again and knocked on the door. This time, Belletrist was the only one there with her child, by the way, about a year old. The child was asleep, so that was good.

This is where it gets into the thick of the fraud ring labyrinth. As with all visits, I asked to be able to do a tour of the house, and she was willing to give me a tour of the house. This was a big house; of course, the big guy had lived there while doing fraud. This is a $450,000 home easily, a large brick house, and new construction.

She took me on a tour. There was a small bedroom downstairs, and then we went upstairs to the main bedroom. Now, we went through the whole house, but as we walked through the home, I saw her clothes and a suitcase in the main closet. This suitcase happened to be open.

I took a look and saw photographs of children I learned were also hers. Belletrist said the children were hers. But there were no children in the house other than the infant. I asked her who the gentleman was in the pictures, and she said that that person was her landlord. I noted that there was a name tag on this suitcase, a female name with the same last name as Belletrist.

I asked her, "Whose name was on the suitcase?"

She said, "I don't know. I told you, that's my landlord's suitcase. I'm watching it for him."

I said OK, and we went downstairs. We were sitting at the kitchen table and again like I always say, *let people tell their story,* whatever story they may want to tell. We started talking about her husband, her children, and the landlord. And this gets crazy fast. Belletrist's husband was working out of town. He's a U.S. citizen (USC).

I'll give her landlord the generic name John Smith. He was born on July 1, 1980. I noted that her ex-husband or husband, also named John Smith, was born on July 1, 1981. I further noted to her that they both looked similar. We discussed this for a few minutes, and Belletrist said, "Well, John Smith 1980 was the brother of John Smith 1981. Remember the twin stories? She said they had the same father but different mothers."

To try to clarify, John Smith 1980 and John Smith 1981 are the same people. Also, the John Smiths. Are you confused yet? Well, welcome to Immigration 101.

Regardless, John Smith 1981 was her husband; however, Belletrist claimed that John "Older Brother" Smith 1980, was the father of her children. And her story (most likely fabricated) was that John Smith 1981 could not have children. They all got together and agreed that Belletrist would have children with John "Older Brother" Smith in 1980. This gets crazy, I told you.

In 1984, there was a cult classic movie with actor Peter Weller (Robocop), John Lithgow, and Jeff Goldblum called *The Adventures of Buckaroo Banzai in the 8th Dimension*, where all the dimensional/alien immigrants were namesakes of John Bigbooté. I kind of felt like I was in the 8th Dimension on this case; maybe Belletrist saw the movie in a rerun, naming **everyone** with the same name.

After all this confusion, Belletrist looked at me and said, "Now, Officer Lee, I know you think I'm lying."

I told Belletrist, (We're not allowed to ever tell anyone that they're lying). "I'm not calling you a liar. I'm simply telling you that I'm confused. Doesn't make sense to me. Please, could you make your explanation make sense to me?"

I asked her to call her USC husband, the older guy.

Belletrist called him. She claimed USC's husband was on the road, traveling out of state. He was helping someone move to another state and being paid for it. That was kind of confusing. They were on the phone. They talked. But he didn't really know where his friend was moving to (maybe the 8th Dimension as well).

As we talked, Belletrist wanted to tell a story a lot of times. When you deal with people, if they don't have a good story or they can't answer a question, they'll go off on a tangent, and this was Belletrist. I mean, this is not an exaggeration. In the process of interviewing, you might ask, "Where did you first meet your American husband?"

She would start off by going, "Well, you know, when I was young, and I was a child, I really didn't know my parents, and I was alone all the time. And so I was frightened. And I'm sad today about that."

Belletrist would not answer the question directly asked. This went on repeatedly. With everything you asked Belletrist, she would talk about something else. One of the things Belletrist talked about was her past. As I was asking her questions about her current USC husband, an old guy, Belletrist would start by saying, I've been a single child. She was an only child. That's what made her sad." She married her first husband, John Smith, in 1981, and she had done that because she was an only child. John Smith 1981 was abusive and mean to her because he couldn't have children. And then, when she did have children with his brother, John "Older Brother" Smith 1980, his half-brother with the same name, it was all messed up and messed up Belletrist herself.

I never asked any of those questions. I didn't know. I mean, I was asking about her current husband. Belletrist would go off and say that stuff. Belletrist took my main rule, to allow the interviewee to tell the story to the outer limits.

I went back and started again, asking why Landlord's suitcase upstairs had the same last name as Belletrist.

She then completely changed her story. She put both of her hands up to her head and popped her head like an emoji. "Of course, I know who she is, the name on the suitcase, that's my sister."

I said, "Wait; I don't understand you, Belletrist. When we were upstairs, you said you didn't know who that person was on the tag because it was your landlord's suitcase."

And she sat there and looked at me, and she goes, "I never said any such thing. I never told you that."

I said to Belletrist, I have two witnesses here that will tell you that's exactly what you said. I don't know why you said that. You did not know her, and now she is your sister."

Then I said to Belletrist, "You told me that you were an only child, that you didn't have any siblings. And that was one of the reasons for your depression and the fact that you married the older gentleman."

And then Belletrist's response was, "Well, well. I'm so much older than my other sister that it was like I was an only child."

She told stories that didn't make any sense, and some of them didn't have a rhyme or reason. To give false information on whether she had a sister or not really had no bearing on her adjudication for status and benefit, but it certainly showed her propensity for far-fetched stories.

So it made no sense. In the end, we didn't get to the bottom of anything. She told stories and would not answer a lot of the questions, Similar to the big guy and the tax lady from the Georgia Revenue Girl story. She would give you a story that had nothing to do with the questions you were asking. Now, the nice thing is that I had two officers who were witnesses to this, and we wrote everything down.

I ended up calling both Belletrist and her spouse, old guy, to the immigration office for an interview. The old guy never showed, and my theory that he was homeless was still viable. Belletrist came in by herself. I think she ended up filing for the Violence Against Women Act (VAWA) and an I-360 battered spouse.

This is a common tactic for women who are in fraudulent marriages, especially with homeless African-American men from Atlanta. The VAWA and I-360 were granted most of the time because the African-American men were homeless and recruited as an asset to the marriage fraud arrangers. Most men didn't even know they had police reports or warrants out for them. Often, the immigrant woman would file a claim, get a police report, and then go back and rescind the complaint after the I-360 was filed, of course. I do not know why, maybe for fear of false claims. Maybe to be humane.

But in Belletrist's case, I don't know what happened after she left my office. Was the storytelling Belletrist married to John Smith in 1981, a homeless old guy, or not at all? Who knows? I certainly do not.

I wrote up the fraud scheme and allowed U.S. immigration service officers to make a decision. Quite often, no matter how much fraudulent reporting you did, USCIS (U.S. Citizenship and Immigration Services) was going to grant them a benefit or upgrade in immigration status. I would like to tell you that the government denied these cases, but there's enormous pressure to approve **everyone**. This is one of those cases that I guarantee you she got her benefit and green card status.

Columbus, Georgia Military Fraud

Georgia has several military bases within the state. The largest of those is Fort Benning, where Special Forces and other training goes on. It's a pretty large military base. Enlisted men are targets of a lot of immigration fraud. You know, they're young, they're personable. They just joined the service. Some of them don't think they make enough money. They meet buddies in the community who may need some help. So you can find lots of cases where soldiers and sailors have been involved in marriage fraud.

I am a military veteran myself. I know the pressure and the desire that people have to get off the base. And these young guys want to get off the base. They don't want to have to stay in the barracks. When I was in, it was the same case. There are a lot of advantages to being married, even pretending to be married. People get married in the military to receive an allowance or housing voucher to live off base (called BAQ or BHA). You get a lot of money for living off base. You get extra money for food. You get extra money for housing. It's serious business. Some of the marriage fraud with immigration is intertwined with military benefits and positioning. Some may argue that military personnel deserve every advantage or angle they can get.

I've met a lot of married couples that never lived together. I worked on a few of these cases. It is difficult to get anyone in military criminal investigations to even call me back to discuss them. Many of these crimes go unpunished and are not seriously investigated. The Department of Defense (DOD) did not understand what our agency did and did not care to learn. DOD didn't want to prosecute, like the U.S. Department of Justice (DOJ). I got the sense that they were petrified that this would get out and sully the name of the military, whereas the DOJ was more ideological or political with their reasons not to prosecute. Either way, it's the old sweep-it-under-the-rug routine.

Since I've been out of the service, I've met several EX-U.S. military service personnel who talked about manipulating the system through marriage fraud. This was prevalent in the military. Duty, along with honor, are the foundations of serving in the U.S. military and a country that is the beacon of light for the free world. When I was in the service, I could never even imagine doing something like that. Sure, we all have done wrong things, but I never crossed the line into fraud.

Service personnel were getting a housing allowance to live off base. Certain soldiers do this, with acquaintances or friends getting married to each other. It's a marriage of convenience, so they can both get off-base housing allowances. I didn't know how prevalent this was until I started working for U.S. Immigration. I started talking to veterans, even some of my veteran colleagues who I worked with at U.S. Immigration.

They freely admitted to manipulating the system. A lady I talked to said she met a guy when they were in the service. They both decided to get married because both could get a housing allowance and live off base. They never lived together. They lived on opposite ends of the country. When they no longer needed to be married, they divorced and moved on.

Let me preface some of the cases that I dealt with. I'm going to talk about one particular filing, but I could cite more than 100 in the U.S. state of Georgia alone. I'm stunned that this was going on at the level that it was.

I heard about something that was not an immigration case but interesting. While I was in the process of doing an investigation of some Army guys taking part in immigration fraudulent marriages stationed at Fort Benning, I spoke to one of the judges at the local courthouse who, at one time, had officiated marriages. The judge said he recognized military guys coming in for arranged marriages.

The judge conducted a marriage between two male soldiers. They came to him to get married. Now, they were legally allowed to marry each other. The soldiers were part of the Special Forces branch at Fort

Benning. The judge was certain it was not a legitimate marriage. They were two young men in their early twenties. After the ceremony, when it came time for them to kiss, the judge let them know they could kiss each other. The soldiers were repulsed by the idea that they would kiss each other. The judge told them, "You guys are supposed to be in love, and you got married; now you should show it." They couldn't bring themselves to kiss each other because they weren't gay. They were there to get the Basic Allowance for Quarter (BAQ), and the judge understood that as well as I did.

I did not understand the desire to do this. I loved being on base when I was in the military. I preferred being in the barracks. The swimming pool was outside of my barracks window. It was someplace to be. It was like being in an apartment. When I got married, I was still in the military. You were on a waiting list to get on base, and so I had an apartment outside the base. I received a housing allowance, but it was not enough to cover my rent. I couldn't wait to get on the base. As soon as an opening came for my spouse and me, I jumped to get back on. Everything was on base; the bowling alley, movie theater, grocery store (with discounted food), and Olympic swimming pool. Everything that you could ever want or need. So why live off base? It doesn't make any sense to me.

A couple married in Georgia. The gentleman was in the Army. He was stationed at Fort Benning. He was married to a Nigerian woman who was living in a house up in Gwinnett County, Georgia. The African woman was actually in immigration removal proceedings. The Enforcement Removal Office had some really serious issues with the application, and they did their research. FDNS (Fraud Detection and National Security) was suspicious of the Fort Benning soldier and the Nigerian lady claiming they were living together. So they sent the file back over to USCIS (U.S. Citizens and Immigration Services) for us as immigration fraud detection officers to do an investigation.

This soldier and this Nigerian woman had been married since 2005. She had lived in Gwinnett County since before the marriage. The visa petition was approved, and the file was with the court for anomalies in her application; therefore, she was in proceedings. I first got the case in 2012.

The soldier and Nigerian lady had shown up to court. They brought documents to support their marriage legitimacy. The Enforcement Removal attorneys noted that the soldier had added his Nigerian wife to receive health insurance. They showed that they were married, and she had an ID card for the base. Examining their documents closely revealed the insurance and ID card were received a few days before they came in for the court date. Further, she was put on his "Survival Document," so if the soldier unfortunately died, she would get his life insurance. Mind you, they'd been married for some years.

The attorneys dug further and found the Nigerian lady was on all of his documents after they first filed their immigration documents many years ago. More baffling, the Nigerian lady was removed from all the soldier's documents a short period after their marriage and original immigration interview. We couldn't understand why the soldier put her on all his military documents when they first married; then he took her off of everything. Then, right before she came into court, the soldier re-added his Nigerian spouse back onto all his important documents, plus she received a highly secured military base ID of her own. The attorneys believed the married couple never lived together. The Nigerian lady had never moved with him as a soldier to any of the military bases that he was assigned.

I began my investigation and did some research to determine where the Nigerian spouse lived, where the soldier lived, and if they had any link whatsoever together. My investigation and research revealed the Nigerian woman had bought a house, the house she was living in. The house that they claimed they shared. She had bought the house with another man! The other gentleman was her African husband; on paper, her ex-husband, which is a common switching-around technique in immigration fraud. All of the ex-husband's (actual husband in reality) information pointed to him living with his ex-wife (actual wife in reality). Further, the African husband had a business he ran out of the Nigerian lady's house.

I gathered what I could and decided it was time to go and do a site visit to the home. My colleague and I went out early in the morning. She was home, and as U.S. immigration officers, we showed our credentials.

We asked if we could go in and talk to her, and the Nigerian lady agreed and allowed us into the house. She led us to the sitting room.

When you first entered the house, there was a room to the left. There was a couch and a couple of chairs in there. It was set up to entertain guests. There was one photo on it, a coffee table. The photo was of the soldier (spouse) in his uniform sitting there. I asked her to give me a tour of the house and show me around. We went through the kitchen, we went through some of the other rooms, and it was a nice home. She showed me the closet where they supposedly kept their clothes. One soldier's dress uniforms hung in the closet. Photos and clothing are good signs the soldier and Nigerian lady were indeed married. Of course, a slick immigration attorney could tip them off to set those items up in case of inspection.

Now, this soldier was a big guy. He was probably a good 6'2", 230 to 240 pounds. She showed me all the other male clothes in the closet as well. The interesting thing is that the soldier's uniform appeared to be a match and would have fit him, but all the other male clothes in the closet were for someone smaller in size. Certainly, didn't seem big enough for a man 230 to 240 pounds and over six feet tall. I'm going off of the photos that I saw of him and the details from his driver's license.

We talked a little bit, about the Nigerian spouse, myself, and my FDNS partner. Apparently, according to her, the soldier had been there that previous weekend. He had left to go back down to Fort Benning. She claimed that he lived down in the Columbus area during the week, and he came home about every other weekend to stay with her. He was a busy soldier, and he didn't have a lot of time. She claimed that she stayed in Gwinnett County because that's where her job was, and her children went to school there. She had two teenage children at the time, not related to the soldier.

Now, limited time with your spouse in the military is not unusual. I've known lots of people who are married to soldiers. They come home when they can. That is not a terrible red flag. But an ex-spouse running a business out of your home. That is a red flag.

I asked her about her ex-husband and why he was on her home documents. "Why does he run a business out of your house?" She said that they were still friends. He was the father of her children. So, he used her home as his business address. It was a place for him to store some of his business equipment.

When I have these kinds of site visits, I'll go and talk to the neighbors. You get more information from the neighbors than you get from the people themselves. You might find out some information you didn't know. Once we left her, my FDNS partner and I looked for some friendly neighbors.

We were coming out of the house, and we were getting in our car. I noticed that the lady who lived to the left of the home was walking out of her own house and getting into her car. So, we walked over to talk to her about the Nigerian lady and the soldier. She was in a bit of a hurry. She was on her way to work. I didn't want to take a lot of her time. I asked if she knew her neighbors.

She said that the couple moved into the neighborhood when it was brand new. Their house was the third house built in the neighborhood a month after they moved in. The Nigerian lady, her husband, and kids began living next door. I showed a photo of the soldier and asked the neighbor if she knew him.

The neighbor said she had never seen him in her life. The neighbor said that she knew the woman and the man. I showed a picture of the African ex-husband. The neighbor knew him as the husband and the father of her two teenage children. She was able to describe them. She said that they were friendly. She had known them ever since they moved in; they were great parents, and their children were amazing kids.

This neighbor was in a hurry, so she asked me to talk to her husband, who was in the house. He was willing to talk to me as well. He came to the door, and I started discussing the same thing with him. I repeated the questions and showed photos of the woman who lived next door.

Her husband gave me the same response. A month after they had moved into their house, the Nigerian lady moved in next door. The neighbor's husband told us they were an African couple. They had two children. He was able to identify the two people who lived in the house through photos that I showed him, and he'd never seen the soldier, didn't know who he was, and never talked to him in four or five years of living there.

They were able to describe the African man who lived there. They knew what he did for a living. They knew what company he ran out of the house. They had seen him with the children and thought he was a good father.

I reached out to the soldier after the site visit interview at the Nigerian lady's house. The soldier said that he was at Fort Benning. He sounded like he was driving. He told me that he was being deployed to Afghanistan. At that moment, his unit was being driven to the airplane to go to Afghanistan. I was not able to talk to him about the case. There was nothing I could do at the time. This is another reason a lot of people like to let these things slide: the soldier's going into harm's way. Many people say, "Who cares what he's doing with a marriage? The soldier's killing terrorists in Afghanistan, let it go."

I wrote up my report and did my summary, laying out the details of what I'd found in this case. I sent the information and findings to the Enforcement Removal attorney.

But that's not the end of the story either.

I should give you a little more background first. This Nigerian lady who was married to our Fort Benning soldier had married two other soldiers from South Georgia. She married one soldier who was from Fort Stewart. Another one again from Fort Benning. Then she ended up marrying her last soldier, who I've detailed in this story. These were rapid-fire marriages. It all started in 2002.

To be fair, the first soldier she married was from Fort Stewart, and the Nigerian lady married him when he was out of the service. The veteran was working as a deli man. This marriage didn't last long. He filed immigration paperwork for her, but I don't think the marriage was six months along before they split. That gentleman was from the Auburn/ Montgomery area of Alabama. I actually couldn't find anything more about him, "parts unknown," as the expression goes.

She married another soldier at Fort Benning for a year or two. Fort Benning's husband (number one) again filed for her, but they ended up getting divorced before the immigration process went through. That gentleman ended up leaving Fort Benning and went out to California and was stationed there. I could not determine if he and the Nigerian lady ever lived together.

I had heard rumors and stories about people on military bases who helped arrange some of these immigration marriages. The story goes that one of the immigrants who joined the military convinced his buddies to marry his sisters, other family members, or friends. Quite a few immigrants join the military. You hear rumors about people helping out their buddies. But this soldier's story was the one that got me to investigate these types of fraud. I found out through some of the interviews that a guy at Stewart was arranging these marriages and helping people out. I ended up with a few of these cases.

In 2016, the soldier's case came back to me from Immigration Enforcement and Removal. After the information I provided, the U.S. attorneys were getting ready to bring this lady back in for another hearing before the immigration judge. But they didn't think it was sufficient. It's a challenge to get enough evidence to declare marriage fraud as opposed to there being just a marital issue.

One of the things I think they wanted me to do was to reach out to the last soldier from Fort Benning and our original guy in this story again and talk to him about this marriage to get his side of the story outside of the courtroom. I agreed and decided to go out and do another site visit, talk to them again, and see if I could get some more information.

I did three more site visits to the home, trying to reach out to the couple. The first time I went out, I showed up at the house, hoping someone would be home around 3:00 in the afternoon. I had some information that the African ex-husband who lived there usually got home at about 2:30 p.m. I ended up getting to the house around 2:00 p.m. We hung out in the neighborhood to see if we could see a flow of people coming in and out of the house. As we were sitting there, I saw a teenager coming up to the house. I went and started talking to him. This teen was the son of the Nigerian lady and African ex-husband who may have lived at the house. He was a little bit nervous. He said that his parents didn't live together anymore; his real father lived somewhere else in another state. He could not tell me which state. He said that the soldier was married to his mother. He could not remember when the soldier he was last at home. He gave me the best story he could.

He was a sixteen-year-old kid. I didn't want to overly push him or anything. I asked him some general questions. He gave me a story, and I let him go into the house. I didn't want to pressure him or scare him. I didn't see any need for that. He was a minor, so I let him go. I could not use a lot of what he said beyond to get some bearings.

I went to talk to the other neighbors, and they were both home. The couple that lived to the right were retired. They both lived in the house. They were from Florida originally.

Their story was similar to the neighbors who lived to the left of the house. The folks on the right had moved in at the same time as the Nigerian lady and African ex-husband couple. They knew them well. They knew their names when they were shown photos of them. They knew their children. They talked about what great parents they were. They had been living next to this couple for ten years. I showed the picture of the soldier. They said they'd never seen him before.

I went to the Nigerian spouse's house two other times. Once was later in the evening to see if I could find who was there. The second time was in the middle of the night at 3:00 a.m. I chose those times based on information I got from the neighbors. They said the African ex-husband left early in the morning to go to work, usually around three or four in the morning, and then he came home, usually around 2:00 p.m., in time for the kids to come home from school. At two or three in the morning, I am not knocking on the door. My fellow officer and I sat across the street from the house and waited to see if anyone came out and went to work. Oddly, no one ever came and went to work.

I never was able to get in touch with either the Nigerian spouse or anyone else in the house after that. No one would come to the door, no one would talk to me, and no one would answer the phone. I was pretty much shut out and out of luck after that.

Because the African ex-husband was in the house and I had at least been in the house, this created a link to the case; therefore, I was able to open up an investigation on the African ex-husband. What I found out about this gentleman was that he was using a different name. I was able to pull records. He changed his name a lot. Not legally; he was just using a different name. Different date of birth. This is not uncommon. I found driver's license information on him with two different names and dates of birth.

I tried to find the soldier again. It'd been three or four years since the last time I talked to him. This time, when I did research, I found he was stationed in Kansas. I decided to dive even deeper and was able to reach out to his command. I talked to a lady who was an Officer Lieutenant in the Army.

What I found was the soldier went back and forth with his Nigerian wife, putting her on federal documents and then taking her off of his documents. Right after I finished my first time looking into the couple, the soldier went back and took her off of all of his life insurance documents and put his mom back on, and he continued to go back and forth, taking the Nigerian woman off and putting her on his crucial documents. He lived in an apartment by himself in Kansas. His neighbors had never seen the Nigerian woman. She never came to visit him, as far as they knew.

I also found other interesting information when the soldier joined the Army. He joined the Army with a good friend, and they shared an apartment in Pennsylvania. The soldier's roommate and good buddy became the second U.S. husband of this Nigerian woman. So she had been married to one of the soldier's friends as well.

I found information from the soldier's mom living in Pennsylvania. I was able to obtain his mom's address and phone number, I gave her a call. I asked her some basic questions, along with confirming it later. She was his mother. She knew about him. She knew he was in the Army. She had not seen him in a year, but he usually came home every year to visit her.

I asked her the last time her soldier son was home, if he had brought his wife home with her. She was completely shocked. She knew nothing about a wife. She goes, "What are you talking about? A wife. He's not married."

I ended up explaining to Mom, "Yeah, he is married. He's been married for more than ten years."

I think, at the time, she knew nothing about this. Understandably, Mom got nervous about the situation. I'm a U.S. immigration officer, and when I told her this, she was worried about the secret life her soldier son was living and if he was in some kind of trouble. I gave Mom some more details: I explained how long her soldier son was married and where they claimed to live.

She didn't know what her son was doing. She told me to talk to him about his marriage.

I agreed. I said thank you very much and let her go. I at least understood that the soldier was married for more than ten years, kept it mostly quiet, and even his mother knew nothing at all about the marriage.

I ended up talking to his command several times. I spoke to the lieutenant over him. His command told me he had some financial issues before with the military, and there was some stuff going on there. I ended up explaining to her that he had been getting a housing allowance for ten years and was pretending to be in a real marriage to a Nigerian woman.

He had probably received $180,000 or more based on his marriage to this woman. That's just the housing allowance that he got. I don't know how much he would get if you totaled all the benefits. He was also allowed extra money for a food allowance since he was married. When I was in the service thirty years ago, you received about 120 dollars a month for food when married.

His lieutenant seemed concerned about what the soldier was doing and what was going on. We talked a couple of times. Each conversation got a little shorter. I got a sense that somewhere up the food chain, she was getting pushback. She could not tell me that specifically, but I sensed it. In the end, the conversations and information flow were cut off entirely by the lieutenant. I don't know what happened.

I gathered up the information that I could and wrote another report on what I'd found. I provided the Immigration attorney with new documents that showed the soldier manipulating his military records to appear as if he was in a legitimate marriage and living with the Nigerian lady. I did everything I could to be fair and accurate.

I know it can be as frustrating to you as it is to me. We don't always know what the outcome is. In this story, we're scrutinizing an enlisted man, and it's tough to do that knowing the danger and sacrifice they go through for our country. We play our part. We do our job. We have our role in this adventure of immigration. If some of these stories appear to be frustrating, and it appears there isn't any closure, what I would say is, "Welcome to the club." It's what I lived with for twenty years as a U.S. immigration officer. You never get to see the full outcome of it. You do your part and do the best you can, but we don't get to see all the roles of the prosecution or outcomes. Everything is hidden behind certain smoke and mirrors, and even the people who work for U.S. Immigration don't see the end all the time.

I've seen more and more female soldiers marry foreign nationals. Most marry foreign nationals from Middle Eastern countries. Happens a lot. I previously mentioned a Nigerian man marrying a U.S. female soldier; Nigeria's population is half Muslim, with the dangerous terrorist group Boko Haram headquartered in Nigeria. Lots of people come into this country from Nigeria; quite a few of them join the military, and some marry into the military for access.

I have so many stories about the military that I'm not sure that I can tell them all, and I don't want to keep hammering away at this. But I do want you to understand the dangers along with the leaders of our country.

I would like to share one more aspect of the military, especially Fort Benning that concerned me. During my time as a U.S. Immigration Supervisor, we had a program called the *Military Accession Vital to National Interest Program,* or MAVNI for short.

This program allows individuals whom the military considers to be of vital interest to the United States easy access to our military. Usually it allowed for fast-tracking of language specialists (translators) and sometimes experts in the medical field. You'll hear the heroic stories of translators, especially in Afghanistan, who fought alongside our troops. This also applies to the military stateside for immigrants to get easy access to our military.

Let me give you an idea of the way it works; I'll give you a simple rundown. A foreigner comes into the country in July as a visitor or a tourist under a B-2 Visa. After August and September, the guy decides to join the Army. He signs up; he's in the military. He goes through boot camp. At the end of boot camp, he is automatically made a U.S. citizen. We naturalize him. And that's what I did, I went down and naturalized these individuals. The foreigner could say, "I came into the country to visit Disney World, I pivoted to join the Army, and in a total of five months, I'm a U.S. citizen."

The fact of the matter is that some of the people they wanted were language specialists in Farsi (Iran) and Urdu (Pakistan). Afghans who knew Pashto, Uzbek. Balochi and Turkmen. Any of those languages would get you in the door quickly. If you had a background in medicine and nursing, you were also in.

I had people who came in July and were finishing boot camp in November. If they did a background check on these individuals and found anything out about them, it would be amazing. It's bullshit. They didn't do a good background check because it was impossible. You can't tell me that they did great background checks; some of these people were from India. Try to get good documentation from India. You should see some of the photos, the way villages store and keep individual information. In some of the villages, it's ridiculous. I don't know how they find anything except on rare occasions. Additionally, your local village away from the U.S. military in Afghanistan doesn't have a database either.

We simply don't know who these people are. I was down at Fort Benning doing a "Welcome to America, you're a Citizen" naturalization ceremony prep. I reviewed everyone's files, records, and documents to determine whether they got everything in order. If there was anything questionable, I wasn't allowed to bring it up. I wasn't allowed to raise a red flag. And I say that with certainty because I tried in the past.

I had a gentleman who came into the U.S. claiming that he was from India. He had gone through boot camp. He was not Indian, not even close to being from India. He was Nigerian. I'm talking to him. He doesn't speak Hindi. He is from Nigeria. And I raise a red flag about this. I called my office regarding this guy who's about to be sworn in as a naturalized U.S. citizen.

I was flat-out told that the DOD, and in particular, the U.S. Army had gone through the process of an investigative background check, and he was good to go. I needed to leave it alone. The issue would not be taken up any further. I shut my mouth, and I finished that off and naturalized him. No one cared.

I still think about military immigration fraud and the apathy around it. Keeps me up at night, folks.

On the immigration side, in the same courthouse, talking to the clerk of the court, they had several of these fraudulent marriages. One marriage the clerk found interesting, and I thought it was interesting as well. An Army U.S. citizen had married a Nigerian guy out of Atlanta. Several months passed, and the clerk received a call from the female in the Army who had married the Nigerian man. She was calling to ask for the man's name and address. She could not remember whom she had married and where he lived. She needed to get in touch with him. The clerk explained that the county could not provide the information over the phone. The female in the Army had to come into the office to get a copy of the marriage application.

G-2 Visa Fraud, Part 1

Let's start out by talking about another big case that I worked on involving G-2 visa fraud. G-2 visa holders are individuals from other countries who've applied to come into the USA under INA section 101(a)(15)(g). What the heck does that mean? INA is the *Immigration and Nationality Act of 1952*. Those eligible are members of accredited organizations and individuals working with our allied governments or non-government organizations (NGOs). So, my G-2 visa fraud case dealt with Nigerian nationals entering the U.S. using G-2 visas under the auspices of working to fight climate change.

The G-2 Nigerians were either in meteorology or they were working in farming, any profession that might avert the impact of climate change. These G-2 Nigerians were supposed to be affiliated with an agency or institution within Nigeria. Conferences were going on in the United States, and the G-2 Nigerians were coming here as a group to participate in important training or lectures to save Planet Earth.

One of the patterns you see in immigration fraud: if hucksters see legitimate work done in a field that spawns a significant number of Nigerian visas for travel to the U.S., then the fraudsters in Nigeria hop right in and try to ride the coattails of legitimate travelers from their country. The distinguished G-2 visas were not immune from the scammers.

I worked on this case with the U.S. Department of State Diplomatic Security Special Agents and CBP (Customs and Border Protection). I worked with the Department of Homeland Security (DHS). There were a lot of us involved in this case within our agency. There were hundreds of erroneous G-2 visas issued in the case.

To give you the basic scheme: Individuals would submit letters from the government of Nigeria saying they worked for some organization or as part of a delegation of people coming here to go to a conference, usually in New York City, Chicago, or Minneapolis. The scam was to get the fraudulent Nigerian G-2 visa holders into the United States. Once they got into the U.S., they could find a U.S. citizen to quickly marry them, and then they could stay forever. A large majority of these individuals, after arriving in the U.S., immediately took domestic flights or buses to Atlanta, Georgia. The G-2 visa scam was a successful method. They had figured out a gaping hole to easily get into the U.S. To make matters worse, there were people within the Nigerian government assisting in the scam. Nigerian government officials created fraudulent letters from their government agencies claiming the applicants were part of various academic and environmental organizations.

Beyond this case, we found systemic fraud throughout the whole G-2 visa process. As I said, the faux G-2 Nigerians came to attend a conference in New York, Chicago, or Minneapolis; however, they always ended up in Atlanta.

So the first question I would ask the immigrant newlywed G-2 visa holder is, "How did you end up in Atlanta when you were fighting climate change in New York, Chicago, or Minneapolis? How did you end up married to a U.S. citizen in Atlanta?"

I knew these were all arranged marriages. They were already set up. They knew to come to Atlanta. That's where they were going to get married. They had to show up in the Peach State (Georgia).

Since this was highly successful, the floodgates opened on G-2 visa applications. Someone got approved using this scam. So, a lot of scammers used the same story. As we now say in society, it went viral. Here are some of the minutiae of the scheme. The fraud story goes, "I came to New York City to attend this conference on a G-2 visa. I flagged down a taxi driver at the airport. By mistake, I entered a taxi; unbeknownst to me, it was a regular car, and when I got in the car, they robbed me of everything."

I do not doubt that somewhere in a city, crimes like this happen. And you could read those accounts in a newspaper. Probably, some crime did occur. But almost every time I spoke to a G-2 visa holder upgrading their status via marrying a U.S. citizen, they all said they got robbed in a fake taxi or robbed on the street.

The story goes: "After I was robbed, I was dumped out on the side of the street in downtown NYC." After, the G-2 visa holder gathered themselves and stood on the side of the street in dismay, distraught, afraid, shivering, and scared. A Nigerian would come up to them, and they would start talking to the Nigerian. And they were so happy that they had met another Nigerian on the street who was willing to help them. And that Nigerians would befriend them and give them some money, then tell them where the bus station was. They would guide them to the bus station and give them enough money to grab a bus ticket to take the bus to Atlanta. The reason they came to Atlanta was they had an uncle, cousin, brother, Sister, niece, and some family members in Atlanta. This was an amazing journey!

I heard it dozens of times.

The next question I would ask G-2 visitors was, "Wait a minute. You came here with a delegation to go to a conference. You have a hotel room in New York City. All your expenses were paid. Your food is taken care of. Your housing is taken care of, and your drinks are taken care of. Why would you go from New York to Atlanta instead of going to your conference? Why not get your boss or let your boss know that you were robbed?"

The common reply by the G-2 visitor was, "I was embarrassed that I was robbed." Or, "They couldn't help me. I didn't know how to get to the hotel."

"But you knew how to get to the bus station, and you couldn't ask someone how to get to the hotel?" "I was in shock over being mugged."

Mind you, this story was fairly common. It happened to everyone, supposedly. I was amazed at how many Nigerians who came to G-2 visa conferences on climate change were robbed.

In my investigation, I would contact the conference because the conferences were real. These climate change conferences did occur. When I would contact the people who were managing these conferences, none of them had ever heard of any of these people. I mean, they had rosters of the people who were coming, the delegations that were coming—they knew who was coming to these conferences, and they were scheduled and prepped for that conference pass that was paid. Not one, not a single one, was ever on any of those guest lists. Out of the hundreds of people that I dealt with, not one.

USCIS Nebraska Service Center Fraud Department contacted the Nigerian government with all of the letters that were on official government papers. Not one of the letters was valid. They were all fraudulent. And as I said earlier, they were set up and created by high-ranking government officials to expedite the scam. But the actual head of the delegation knew nothing of the people coming.

The G-2 visa visitor, now a petitioned immigrant, would come to the office married to a U.S. citizen. They met and fell in love, mostly in a month or less. Paris is no longer the City of Love; Atlanta, Georgia, has taken the crown. They couldn't find the conference to see their boss, but they could meet a lady or man in Atlanta in a day and tie the knot. If they were previously married in Nigeria, they quickly filed for divorce in Atlanta. This is a fast process. This is not years. This is a couple of months. About six months after their divorce, we got the freshly divorced immigrant, now newlywed with a U.S. citizen case in front of us at U.S. Immigration.

When I would interview these individuals as part of the fraud ring, I would ask them about their jobs in Nigeria. What was their background and experience in climate change?

Some would claim to be a meteorologist working in climate or working in agriculture, not as farmers, but as university people dealing with soil testing and conservation and things of that nature. None of them had any clue. They didn't even know the scientific lingo. I asked them about the basic concept of cloud cover or the different levels of the atmosphere. The different types of soil. They couldn't tell me anything. I wouldn't ask traditional interview questions with the G-2 environmentalist, I would Google basic Elementary science issues dealing with either soil geography, topography, or weather. They didn't even know the rudimentary definitions or concepts of any of these fields. The G-2 visa scammers came to the U.S. for Climate Change but only got a change in immigration Status, along with a new U.S. citizen Spouse.

G-2 Visa Fraud, Part 2

This is the second story of the two part G-2 visa fraud. As you remember from the first story, G-2 visa holders are eligible members of accredited organizations and individuals working with our Allied governmental or non-governmental organizations (NGOs). I would be remiss if I didn't tell you one of my intriguing stories. Most of the U.S. agencies were searching for a man who obtained a G-2 visa long ago. The Department of State Diplomatic Security was involved, U.S. Citizenship and Immigration Services, the Department of Homeland Security Investigation, Enforcement and Removal, as well as Customs and Border Protection.

The old APB (all-points bulletin). All the U.S. government agencies were looking for a guy who turned out to be an elusive G-2 visa phantom. Nobody could find him, from all the agencies, until it ended up in my lap. Even the stealthy G-2 phantom needed love, and I searched to see if he had married in the U.S. I found out quickly the G-2 phantom had married. This means he had a file with U.S. Immigration, and I knew we could dig and find his original address. I always wanted to be a Ghostbuster! (That's a great movie with actor Bill Murray.)

The G-2 phantom wasn't *Casper the Friendly Phantom*. He was pretty good at financial fraud, had several bank accounts with different names, and was funneling money back to Nigeria.

As is typical, the G-2 phantom was married to a U.S. citizen. The G-2 phantom originally came down from New York City. The G-2 phantom didn't go to any conferences or any of the stuff that the normal G-2 visa holders go to. He skipped all that and went straight to the interview process for marrying a U.S. citizen in Atlanta. U.S. Immigration had suspicions about the marriage and previously logged signs of fraud.

All the agencies involved in the search coordinated a site visit to his original marriage application address. The place where the G-2 phantom and his wife were supposed to be living. The original application was years ago, so we weren't sure if he still lived at the address.

U.S. Immigration is allowed to do a "bed check" to see if there were any signs the couple were living together; this was our angle for U.S. Immigration to approach and all the other agencies to tag along. I had a new immigration officer who was assisting me on the site visit. She had just started with FDNS (Fraud Detection and National Security). Along with the rookie fraud officer, the multiagency task force included a diplomatic security investigator and a customs and border protection officer, along with the other agencies driving in separate cars. In total, we had eight officers and one special agent going out. We all met up at the apartment location where the G-2 phantom and his wife claimed to be living in the past. We all parked outside of the apartment complex.

We went up, we found the apartment, and the Rookie and I knocked on the door while the rest of the team of officers and agents hung back a little bit.

The G-2 phantom came to the door. I showed my U.S. immigration officer credentials as normal. I told him that we were there to talk to him about his marriage. I asked if we could interview him about that. He agreed to let us in the door. It was about 6:30 in the morning when this happened. We arrived early as we walked in the door. The first thing I noticed was someone sleeping on the outdoor balcony. There's a little cot out there. The gentleman on the balcony wakes up, gets out of bed, and leaves the apartment.

The apartment is a small, two-bedroom apartment. There's a little living room, kitchen, and dining area in the front. And as you come in the door to your left, there is a bedroom. There's another bedroom in the back, and there's a bathroom, but for now, we're in his bedroom. This ended up being his bedroom in the front, and I asked the G-2 phantom if his U.S. petitioning spouse was there, and he said no. Her uncle had died, and she had gone to see him. A common theme and answer—I heard a lot of stories of uncles dying. Pretty much all the time in immigration. Another one of those things where, "Hey, this dead uncle story works," and it's disseminated through the scammer grapevine. People don't want to mess with you when some family member dies. But you want the death to be distant enough so you don't have to be too distraught. Right? When it's touchy, like a parent dies as opposed to an uncle, it's tough to fake that.

The G-2 phantom (or ex-phantom) let me look in the bedroom, and there's nothing there that would suggest a female spouse resided at the apartment. No female clothes in the closet. There's nothing at all in the bathroom that would show that a female is there. There are no feminine hygiene products. There's one toothbrush in the bin. This is a single-person bedroom. I only do this because the bedroom is so close to the front door. We go into the living room, and we sit down at the kitchen table. I asked him if anybody else was in the home.

He stated that no one else was in the home. For my own safety, for my rookie partner's safety, and for the others that could come in later, I asked if he didn't mind showing me around the apartment.

He agreed. I asked him to show me the other bedroom. As soon as he opened the other bedroom door, I saw two men standing in the bedroom. And I'm like, *Whoooaa,* a little scared, a little bit nervous. I could've been *slimed,* like in the *Ghostbusters* movie. He had told us there was no one else in the home. These two gentlemen appeared like spiritual entities themselves.

I asked the two gentlemen to come out of the bedroom, and they did. I asked the G-2 phantom if I could look at the bathroom. The G-2 phantom agreed to let me enter the bathroom. This is the second bathroom because there's a bathroom in his room, we already checked out. Well, he opened the door for me into the bathroom.

And I noticed that the curtain on the bathtub was closed but rustling; *there must be another phantom in the house.* This time, I actually pulled back the curtain because I was a little bit nervous. When I did, I saw five Nigerians standing back-to-back. In the bathtub, hiding. Quite frankly, this made me a little bit irritated. I got on him about that there were all these people in the house when he had said there's no one else there.

And he was unapologetic for the most part. We get all of these men to go out and sit in the living room, and we're talking to them a little bit, but they're all belligerent. Actually, they don't want to talk to us. And I'm fine with that. I didn't come there for them. I tell them that I'm not here for them. The G-2 phantom is the only one that I know who's filed any U.S. Immigration paperwork. And that's what I'm there about. I tell them they're free to leave because they want to leave, and a couple of them are Canadian citizens. They were all born in Nigeria, but a couple of guys were naturalized as Canadian citizens.

Often, you'll have five or six of these guys living in one apartment, and they're all part of a financial fraud scheme. The G-2 phantom was the crew boss, and they all worked together using fraudulent identities. They opened a ton of bank accounts, as many as they could, and they funneled small amounts of money through these accounts. They do tax fraud, credit card fraud, Green Dot debit card fraud, and FEMA fraud. Our investigation showed in the long run, these gentlemen were all part of the same racket.

All the other men left and went downstairs to the parking lot. CBP went down and talked to the guys that left the apartment, examining their identities. They had an interest in them that I didn't.

I talked to the G-2 phantom about his visa. It was a typical G-2 visa, the same story that we spoke about in the first G-2 visa fraud story. The G-2 phantom parroted the usual con: I came to New York, got robbed, and didn't know anyone there. The G-2 phantom had an uncle in Atlanta. The uncle that would eventually support him after the faux robbery in NYC. The G-2 phantom then met a lady on the street in New York who was from Nigeria, and she ended up helping him out and giving him some money to come down to Atlanta. Typical story. I've heard this scam story repeated over and over again.

The G-2 phantom's trek to Atlanta was based on a fictitious story. Was his marriage a sham as well? His U.S. citizen wife wasn't at the apartment;

a guy was sleeping on the porch, the G-2 phantom, two guys were in the back bedroom, and five dudes in the shower.

We finally tracked down the G-2 phantom's wife at another location, and she told us the marriage was a fraud and helped us prove their fake marriage. She'd been paid to enter the marriage with the G-2 phantom. Now, that wasn't a surprise.

This G-2 phantom visa case was primarily a Department of State case, and I will tell you, I worked a lot of those cases. We found a lot of fraud in this one. We discovered a lot of fraudulent documents. The roots of these rackets are unbelievable and run deep. In the G-2 phantom case, we eventually found out all his crew were a part of the fraudulent schemes ... when they weren't busy huddling in the shower together.

Shockingly, the G-2 phantom's racket was supported by some high-ranking Nigerian officials. Once that level of diplomatic sensitivities was determined, this G-2 fraud case disappeared like a phantom into thin air. The G-2 phantom case was sent to Washington, D.C. headquarters. To my knowledge, no one was ever prosecuted in a criminal court, not in Atlanta, anyway. If they did something, they were supposed to be prosecuted in Washington, D.C.

The U.S. Diplomatic Security Agent that I worked with was assigned a post overseas, and I never heard anything more about the G-2 phantom case again. The case was buried deeper than a corpse in the scary graveyard. It's typical. You see, a lot of these cases involving sensitive issues with another government just vanish in thin air.

As frightening as the G-2 phantom financial fraud case was to American taxpayers, the Nigerian government's fear of embarrassment trumped the needs of hardworking Americans. The Nigerian and U.S. governments wanted the G-2 phantom case swept under the rug. The G-2 phantom, as a person, was easy to locate, but the larger racket directly tied to top officials in the Nigerian government was more elusive and disappeared into the night just like that.

After the Border

Black Mayberry, Part 1

This is another two-part story. I consider the case a great experience for me as a person and a U.S. immigration officer. It is a fraud case, but there's some real humor in it with interesting twists.

Two immigrants from an African country were together at some point, and they met two African-American U.S. citizens.

In 2014, I was assigned an immigration case with an African male and female. The African male was from Ghana and married a U.S. citizen, an African-American female from a small town south of Tuscaloosa, Alabama.

The guy from Ghana and the lady from Alabama met in the year 2000. Apparently, the Ghanaian male worked with the Alabama female's sister in Atlanta. The Alabama woman came up to visit her sister in Atlanta and introduced the guy from Ghana. Now, the sister in Atlanta actually married another man from Ghana and helped him to get his green card and process it through the system. This is a common theme. Families get other family members involved. *Hey, I got an easy 2,000 bucks. You can also get an easy 2,000 bucks.* That's kind of the way it goes, or $500, or whatever the market bears. And they get a finder's fee, right? Think apartment-referral type of setup. The sister probably received a finder's fee for bringing someone else to the table. Very common. If you go to an apartment complex and you bring someone else, you get a free month's rent. Well, immigration fraud is no different. If you bring somebody else, you either get a discount or you get a referral or a finder's fee. And this was pretty common.

When I was doing my investigations, I had to track all of the parties down. It was easy. It's always easiest if you can find the person who lives closest to your office, and in this case, the guy from Ghana appeared to live closest to my office. I don't want to give away some of our trade secrets but trust me, we can go through database systems using your name, your date of birth, and your Social Security number and find out so much information about you.

Yeah, that's what happened here. I was also looking for a young Nigerian lady. Every time I looked, the guy from Ghana would also pop up. They were sharing addresses and merged with all kinds of data. You may remember the young Nigerian lady and the guy from Ghana were married to two different U.S. citizens and weren't supposed to be connected at all.

That information set me on the path of looking for the guy from Ghana. The first place I looked for the guy was at the address of the Nigerian lady. When you start knocking on all of these doors, you're going see who l ives there and who's on the lease. I asked if anybody knew the guy from Ghana. Now, this case goes back to 2000. So, that's more than twenty-three years ago.

One of the interesting things about apartment complexes is the difficulty in retrieving their rent rolls, who lived in the apartments, and for how long. The apartment complex real estate has a high turnover. In Atlanta, the apartment complex's turnover rate is frequent, about five to ten years. A lot of these apartment complexes only keep records for a certain number of years, usually five to seven years. Some of the places the immigrants claim to live are never going to have records to contradict their stories. I've heard it all from apartment managers and owners: Oh, the files were in storage down in the basement, or the files were somewhere else. Sometimes no records are even kept. It was like pulling rhinoceroses' teeth to find any information.

The first place I even got a hint on the whereabouts of the guy from Ghana was, in fact, an apartment complex. One of the things you can do is take subpoenas to try to compel people to give you information. You usually get a lot of good information from the landlord. They know the comings and goings in homes, who is there, and who is not.

I showed up at the property manager's office with my subpoena, photos, and information pertaining to the actual lease for the apartment complex from the guy from Ghana and his American spouse's application. I talked to the landlord in the leasing office, and, like most people, we always had a good conversation. You want to chat; you want to put their minds at ease. I received confirmation that the guy from Ghana and his American citizen wife were on the lease. Next, I showed a photo of the U.S. citizen spouse to the property manager.

The landlord said he saw a lot of African males come in and out on a daily basis. in terms of the guy from Ghana's female relationships, the landlord saw many random women come and go, and the property manager's team coined the term "love nest" to refer to the guy from Ghana's appetite for women.

I began to suspect that his African-American female spouse was fraudulently married. So I pulled out a picture of the African American spouse, and I asked, point blank, have you ever seen this woman at the apartment? The married couple was supposed to be living in the apartment complex. The landlord was adamant they had never seen the African American female there ever in the two years of the guy from Ghana's lease. From the database leads associating the Nigerian lady with the guy from Ghana, I showed the landlord the Nigerian lady's photo. Both the landlord and property manager agreed that they had seen the Nigerian female at the apartment, and she was using the name of his American wife. The Nigerian lady was faking being the American spouse of the guy from Ghana, a clever but risky move. To pile on further criminal charges, the Nigerian lady was also forging the name of his American wife. I had further information that led me to believe the Nigerian lady was using some kind of ID showing her as the American spouse. That whole scenario is an example of why you don't want to get involved in marriage fraud: it's a gateway for further crime. The American citizen accomplices get more than they bargain for in trouble and long-lasting issues with identity theft.

Now the interesting thing was the guy from Ghana recently purchased a house in Smyrna, Georgia. He had bought the home three months prior to my investigation. I went to that home several times to try to talk to him. I went early in the morning, sat outside of his house until the sun came up, and waited to see if anyone would come out.

I knocked on the door, and an older man would come to the door, I mean really old, with a walking cane, and he said he'd never seen the gentleman. All right, the older man pretended like he didn't know who the guy from Ghana was, even though I had the records that he bought the house and apparently lived there. I went late at night. After the older man with the cane came to the door on the first visit, every time thereafter I knocked on the door, no one ever came to the door again. They would never answer the door for me. Not much I could do. It ended up being a dead end as far as talking to anyone, and eventually, you have to move on to other leads. There's nothing you can do.

But I didn't want to give up completely. So I started investigating the U.S. citizen spouse to find out where she might live, and this is when I discovered it. She lived in a small town southeast of Tuscaloosa, Alabama. Really country. I enjoyed this part of the story the most; it was a great experience for me.

From my experiences fifteen years ago, I call this town Black Mayberry. This story's title references the two TV shows, *Mayberry RFD* and *The Andy Griffith Show*. They are the epitome of glorified rural life in the South: heavy on family, community, and wholesome moral values. The reason I call it *Black Mayberry* is the small town's friendly folks, atmosphere, and typical, Southern, very well-kept look. The typical Southern town has a square in the center of the town. It's either a little park or it's the courthouse. In this case, it was a little tree-lined park which anchored the beautiful, quaint town in the center, with the shops and stores going along each side of the square. It's almost like *A Wonderful Life,* an inspirational Christmas movie set in a small town.

Many spinoffs of the fictitious town of Mayberry have taken place. I had a friend who used to call an urban rockabilly community with tattoos Mayberry on Acid, with the same throwback sideburns, politeness, manners, and morals as Mayberry but planted in an area of a modern city, with great music and heavy on the ink. This Mayberry-on-Acid phrase has been used to describe other towns as well. *Black Mayberry,* as I called the sleepy small Alabama town, is well-kept and neat, and people walk by greeting each other. It's a slice of Americana at its best. Since those TV shows were almost entirely populated with Caucasians, I thought it was important to let everyone know that Mayberry's small-town way of life is true for all races, and I loved the town in Alabama, so I'm calling this story Black Mayberry to eliminate TV stereotypes from yesteryears. Black Mayberry's overwhelmingly African-American population lives the same small-town lifestyle.

Off on the corner sat the police department and the sheriff's office across from there. I think this town was the county seat as well. From what I could tell, all the sheriffs coming in and out were African American; fortunately, no one emulated the fictitious character Deputy Barney Fife and put me under his silly scrutiny.

I went to the police department because I was trying to find a U.S. citizen married to the guy from Ghana. I don't know this town well or where some of the streets are located. You get out in the wooded areas, and sometimes your GPS doesn't work well. Anytime we go out, we must have someone go with us. And in this case, I didn't bring someone from my office. I've always had good luck with local PD going with me. I figured I would do the same thing in this small town. If that didn't work out, I would try to meet the American wife at McDonald's or whatever restaurants were available.

When I got in there, the police chief was inside. And by the way, there are only two police officers in the town. There's the police chief, and there's a part-time police officer who works about twenty hours a week. The time was the middle of the day, with all the hustle and bustle at the peak hour of the morning. I showed my credentials. I talk to the chief. He's a nice guy, professional. It's one of those odd things where you read a person in the spur of the moment, looking him up and down, talking to him for a few minutes. Thinking, you know, he might've been stuck up. For this small-town job, he's probably not making a large salary. You could tell this is his town, and that's why he's here doing the job. There are people like that in their hometown and in their element. They want to be a part of their home community, see it grow, or make sure it's a good place. The chief was sharp and could've excelled anywhere he wanted. On the other hand, there must have been something that tied him to this sleepy town. It was a similar case; however, the part-time police officer seemed a little more disappointed because he wanted more hours and to have this as his full-time career as an officer in a small town in Alabama.

Even with the restrictions, the part-time police officer was exceptionally professional, nice, and cordial. We had great conversations. We're both veterans, which always creates instant bonding, especially with veterans now working in law enforcement. A lot of officers are veterans. Typical questions that I get from fellow vets in local police are, "How do I get into your job, the federal workforce?"

They didn't have to go and look up the guy from Ghana's wife. Both officers immediately knew who she was. They didn't necessarily know her, like from the church choir. But they knew where she lived: "Go right down off Highway 13, and there's a little house on the right-hand side of the road. Oh yeah, I remember her." Both officers knew about her because the town was small enough, just big enough that they didn't know her really well, but they didn't have to look anything up at a mention of her name. I grew up in this same small-town environment. There's always some nostalgia for us who experienced a little town—part of you wants to move and live there again.

The part-time officer was gracious enough to ride along with me, so we spent time driving down the road, discussing local and federal levels as we were trying to find the American wife. I talked to him about how to get a job with the federal government, tried to encourage and help him, and made sure he had my contact info.

After we arrived at her location (the fifty-something American wife of the guy from Ghana), we could see her house, and she was clearly impoverished. The house was 500 square feet, maybe in total. A small box, a cube with a roof on it. The house sat right on the side of a little gully cliff. Literally, right on the side of the road, there was almost not enough room to park without parking on the road. That's how close the house sat to the road. The house did have a small front Porch. A couple of things. You notice the house was green, kind of dark green. Had two windows in the front. And then a space for a door. There was no door to enter the house, which was odd. The door entrance was covered with this heavy, clear, thick industrial plastic. I knocked on the door, or literally on the side of the house, and a lady came to the front door.

I showed my credentials, and the police officer identified himself and showed his credentials. I explained why I was there and that I worked for U.S. immigration. I asked if she was the lady I was looking for. She said, "Yes, it is." I asked if I could come in and speak to her about her marriage to this guy from Ghana. She agreed, and so we entered the house.

I began to speak to her about her marriage to this gentleman. I asked her if she had filed an I-130 petition for an alien relative for the guy from Ghana, her husband. In fact, she filed three times, and two of them had already been approved. The guy from Ghana had some immigration issues, and so his adjustment was held up because of this, requiring multiple applications or petitions by his small-town wife. One of the I-130 petitions was pending, and that was the reason I made the location visit.

In our conversation, I learned that she had met him, as I previously mentioned, through her sister. The small-town wife came up to Atlanta a few times, one time to meet him and one time to get married. Two other times, she was visiting her sister; finally, the small-town wife came up to visit him because he was in immigration deportation proceedings to be removed from the country. He had brought her up to be with him at court. This was so she could tell the judge that we were married. So she did just that.

I don't want you to think that this lady was somehow evil, wicked, or bad. She was a complete sweetheart. She was so demure. She was so soft-spoken. Clearly, she had a kind heart; however, most definitely in a desperate financial situation. And trusting her sister to not lead her down a really bad path. The Alabama small-town wife told me everything, told me all the heartbreak, all the issues. Why did she do it? She was trying to help him out, but he was also giving her money. She thought it was a good thing to do to help the immigrant. He gave her a sob story about his homeland. Typically, she fell for it, along with the fact that he would send her a little money for her phone bill or help with groceries from time to time.

In this case, she told us under oath in her own handwriting how the guy from Ghana paid her to marry him and how her sister got her involved in the fraud scheme. The number of times she'd gone up there to the big city of Atlanta, and for what reasons she came to Atlanta. And in the fifteen years that they were supposedly married, she had only seen the guy from Ghana three or four times. She had talked to him on the phone every month or so to check in with her faux husband. *Is everything OK?*

And he would send her a little bit of money or pay for her phone bill or something like that. And the small-town wife would call him when she needed a little extra money for food or whatever.

At the end of our conversation, when I was getting ready to leave, I said, "Well, you know, why did you get a driver's license in Atlanta if you never lived in Atlanta? What was your reason for doing that?" She said, "I told his immigration attorney that I didn't live in Atlanta that I actually lived here in the small town of Black Mayberry and always lived here, and this was my home. The attorney told me I needed to get a license in Atlanta so that it looked like I lived in Atlanta, so I went and got a driver's license in Atlanta."

The immigration attorney should have had his bar license taken for that or disbarred.. He's a prominent Attorney in Atlanta, by the way. And a complete jerk, quite frankly.

When I went back to Atlanta, I wrote the case up. This is the part of the movie when the detective or investigators say, *I hate paperwork*, but with the handwritten confession under oath from the small-town wife of the guy from Ghana, I gladly took the time. There's some more detail to it, but for the most part, we had enough. We had enough evidence and information from visiting the leasing office and retrieving documents from the landlord and property manager showing the fraudulent couple didn't live there together. An Immigration Service Officer (ISO) in Atlanta wrote this up as a denial, technically called "an intent to revoke." ISO was going to revoke his I-130 petitions that had been approved. The small-town American wife withdrew one of the filings but not all. These are the complexities of filing. The small-town wife had filed three petitions in fifteen years. After talking to me, she removed one filing that was approved and one pending. There was a third one that had been approved, so we needed to rescind it through U.S. Immigration to make sure that they were all off the books, and that's what Atlanta U.S. Immigration does.

I put a lot of work and effort into this case, so I wrote up a nice blurb to go along with an intent to revoke. "We're going to take your I-130 that was approved away from you because you're not really married. We have sufficient evidence to show that this is a sham marriage." It ended up being a thirteen-page addendum to my report detailing everything that I've done in the case. And all this stuff, all the information in the derogatory witness testimony and information that I found. I wrote it in such a way that they could copy and paste it directly into the letter to rescind his visa petition.

When you send one of these letters to the petitioner's American spouse, you have to give them thirty days to respond, and so it sits on the shelf for a little while. Eventually, the attorney responds for them, which is typical. Also, the attorneys usually will accuse you of the worst things that someone could possibly think of because if they can get a sympathetic judge, a sympathetic jury, or whoever to believe them, then they could throw out whatever you did. In this case, all your work is down the drain.

This attorney wrote how I had threatened his client, had used foul language with her, had been harsh and mean to her, and how the small-town part-time police officer who went with me was intimidating, and she was scared that she was going to be arrested, and I threatened her with arrest. "You'll be arrested during the process." Mind you, I've never threatened anyone in my entire career, and as you read in this story, that filing from the attorney was a pack of lies and slanderous if you were allowed to litigate. I taught in immigration class to other U.S. immigration officers it's dangerous to threaten arrest to someone, and you'll lose your case every time if you do that. So don't do it.

The attorney also claimed that his client, the small-town wife, never said any of her written confessions. Never said that she was paid and never said that they didn't live together, never said that it was all set up and everything was a fraud so that he could stay here and get a green card. She never said any of that stuff, and I (the U.S. immigration officer) was putting words in the intent to rescind that was not true and had been completely fabricated by me. I guess her attorney missed the handwritten confessions outlining all of the accurate details.

Of course, you take this personally when someone is calling you either a liar or saying that you're doing someone harm, and you don't want to let that slide. Your reputation is on the line, and this attorney was a real dirtbag, to say the least. He looked nice all dressed up. He's pro-immigrant to the point of doing anything shady, but we're trained to resist the fog of insults and forked tongues. Again, I helped the ISO write up the response, and I had to go through it all again. You have to go back through when the immigrant's attorney rebutted their own rebuttals. So, you can imagine an intent to rescind can be pretty lengthy, especially with the attorney's added-on detailed rebuttal. And you've got to respond to it.

Well, one of the things that really got me on this case, the attorney had said the small-town wife never said any of this, and none of this ever occurred. The confession was in her own words, in her own handwriting, because as I told you, I wrote the questions out, and I had her hand-write her answers and swear to them. The small-town wife had written out every one of those answers in her own handwriting. I could say, "No, this is her handwriting, not mine." You probably couldn't read my handwriting anyway. I do not know if a response was received after that. I have to assume the filing was denied, and the Ghanaian man was placed in proceedings.

In another interesting development, the guy from Ghana had a child with his younger Nigerian mistress, who I spoke of earlier; the young Nigerian mistress stole the identity of the wife from small-town Alabama.. That's Black Mayberry, part 2, which is interesting as well.

Black Mayberry, Part 2

This is the second part of the Black Mayberry story.

I previously talked about the guy from Ghana who was married to an African-American woman from a small town in Alabama (the embodiment of Mayberry, the fictitious wholesome and sleepy town from *The Andy Griffith Show* in the 1960s).

This is the story of the "Nigerian" female who had a child with a guy from Ghana. I suspect they were actually married in real life, and the guy from Ghana had a fraudulent marriage with the American citizen from small-town Alabama.

This young Nigerian lady was probably twenty or more years younger than the guy from Ghana. The Nigerian lady was his lover. Everywhere I would go to look for the guy from Ghana, her name would pop up. The Nigerian lady's information would pop up through different systems checks, databases, and software algorithms. So they've been living together for some time. Not for the same length of time that he was claiming marriage to the U.S. citizen from Alabama, but for a pretty long time, at least in the United States.

So I did some research and found out the young Nigerian lady was actually in the process of filing for immigration benefits through marriage to another U.S. citizen. As I talked about in "Black Mayberry, part 1," when I showed pictures of the guy from Ghana's U.S. wife, no one in the leasing offices of their previous residences had ever seen her. When I showed pictures of the Nigerian lady, they all knew her as the guy from Ghana's wife. It started to seem like a strange episode of the TV show *Wife Swap*.

Furthering the plot, the landlord and property manager said the same name knew the Nigerian lady as his Alabama wife. We could add some identity theft to the charges one day.

The leasing agents said the Nigerian lady had been in two days before, paying the rent. She also had some questions about the apartment. The landlord stated that she and the guy from Ghana had lived there together for a while. The landlord and property manager also knew the couple had bought a house together in Smyrna, Georgia. The Nigerian lady would still come by to pay the rent. The leasing staff was confused about the whole scene, and they thought the apartment was used primarily by the guy from Ghana and some of his male friends from Africa. You may remember from other stories that it's kind of typical for Nigerians and West Africans to rent an apartment as a placeholder for their friends to come in from the airport as a safehouse. Additionally, the locations were fronts for their coworkers for financial fraud arrangements, identity theft, or whatever the trendy scam was. These guys also used them as play apartments, a place where they could bring women to party and have a good time like Tony Montana from the gangster movie *Scarface* motto: work hard in crime and play harder.

The landlord said the guy from Ghana still came there to entertain other women and friends. I don't know what that arrangement was in full.

They tend to bring in young African girls for prostitution also. You can google Rex Anyanwu to see his convictions. That is another story. As I talked about many times, marriage fraud is a gateway to larger crimes, including human trafficking. You'd find an apartment of African women, these young African girls set up in apartments. Some immigrant pimp kingpin had brought them into a town near you to run them out of an apartment as escorts and prostitutes. It's probably as common as seeing Asian massage parlors down the street, but it's not advertised the same way or as mainstream. It's because immigrant cultures are more linked to their own communities, creating a pipeline to bring in groomed prostitutes.

In this case, I am not sure what all the young Nigerian Smyrna lady was to the guy from Ghana: wife, baby mama, girlfriend, mistress, mule, co-conspirator. I knew they were together at the apartment complex and now at a nice house, together probably worth $250,000 at the time, now $375,000. Big, pretty new home on the cusp of one of the up-and-coming areas of Atlanta.

Some of the research on the Nigerian lady showed that she had married a U.S. citizen, an African-American male who ended up being a homeless guy. He'd been a drug abuser for some time. That is the story I obtained from his family. It's a common technique for marriage arrangers to take advantage of homeless people, knowing U.S. Immigration has difficulty tracking them down.

I spent a lot of time looking for the homeless guy. He was officially married to the Nigerian lady, and her pathway to satisfying the requirements to get a green card. In a marriage like this, a lot of times, they'll send in photographs and images and things of their marriage together. In this case, the homeless guy and the Nigerian lady had sent in photos of themselves with an older woman. I assumed that it was the homeless guy's mother. It looked like he was hugging her. The Nigerian lady was standing there right up against the homeless guy. The thing is that it didn't seem like they were at home, you know, at someone's house. It was a bit sterile, which made me suspicious. The saying goes, a picture tells a thousand words, but this one may have told ten thousand words.

Since I couldn't find the homeless guy in my search for the Nigerian lady, I looked up one of the homeless guy's relatives. I was doing all of this to work my way back to the guy from Ghana and nail him for his marriage fraud. I ended up finding the homeless guy's sister, and I talked to her on the phone. The sister knew nothing about this marriage to the Nigerian lady. But the sister did say, "You know, my brother has had a lot of problems. He struggled for a long time. He's had some drug issues. We don't know where he's at. We hear rumors about him living on the street, and he's at this shelter, or he's over here, and people will see him sometimes walking in the neighborhood. Or through some of the old neighborhood friends that know him." She confirmed that he was a homeless guy destined for the streets from drug abuse.

I explained to the sister that her homeless brother said in his application he was living with his mother and acting as a caregiver. The sister said,

"I could tell you that they never lived in my mother's house because my mother lives in a nursing home, and she lived in a nursing home for many years." That was long before the time of the marriage vows of her homeless brother and the Nigerian lady.

When I finally met with the sister and showed her the photo of the Nigerian lady, the sister had never seen her before. The sister also confirmed the photos were not from their mom's house but from the nursing home she lived in. Bingo!

I was able to get the location and phone number of the nursing home. When I spoke to the people at the senior living center, they wouldn't give out much information. They can't go into detail with people because there are HIPAA laws (Health Insurance Portability and Accountability Act of 1996) that protect patients' privacy and disclosure of their information.

What they could tell me about Mom without getting in any trouble was that she was a resident there. They wouldn't tell me how long she'd been a resident there. Further, I asked: "Does Mom live with anyone? Do her son and her daughter-in-law live here?"

The nursing home staff confirmed to me that they don't live there because they don't allow other non-senior relatives to live there. It was only Mom living there in a one-bedroom apartment. I pretty much understood that this was not a valid marriage for immigration purposes; most likely, it was a full-blown fraudulent relationship with longer tentacles.

I continued doing my research. I focused a lot more on the Nigerian lady. Again, everything came back to her living with the guy from Ghana.. I started looking into the Nigerian lady's entry into the country because a lot of times when people enter the country, they'll say, "Hey, I'm married to John Smith, U.S. citizen" to get into the country. Well, the interesting thing about this young lady is that not only was she committing marriage fraud, but she had used three different names to attempt to enter the country. She'd been denied twice, and the third time, she had been approved.

Now, one of the things about Nigeria is there are two places where you could obtain a U.S. visa. You could either go to the City of Abuja, or you could go to Lagos. A potential immigrant would go to Lagos in an attempt to get a visa. If they were unable to get a visa in Lagos and were denied, they would make the journey to Abuja. They would then apply often with the same name or even a different name. Often, the second time, in the new place, they would be approved. You see this all the time in the Nigerian consulate. It is like the state department officers there never really look at their systems. Or the application denial was not entered into the database fast enough in time to catch the speedy application at the second location. They approve them the second or third time. It was crazy, but that's what they did. She had gone to Lagos, I think twice, and had been denied, with two different names. Nigerians sometimes have four or five names, so technically, it was their name, but they could shuffle the words around or shrink the length of their name. They simply mix them up a bit.

In this case, this is exactly what the Nigerian lady did, but she got turned down on both configurations of her names in Lagos. So, she went to Abuja and used a completely different name. Well, she used a similar name, but she twisted it around a little bit. I think she used the same first name, but she used a completely different last name that didn't show up on any database check. The Nigerian lady was granted and approved a visa to come into the United States on the final try.

I had photographs, I had images. I had all of the visa applications that show this, that she was using three different names. Overwhelming proof of fraud.

Couples will send in photos to U.S. Immigration to prove that they're married. We'll get family photographs, birthdays, Christmas events, and parties, whatever. They like to send pictures in. They'll send pictures of going to Kroger (grocery store) and shopping. Going to the shoe rack and buying shoes, it looks like married couples are doing things together. When I taught fraud classes for U.S. Immigration, I used to say, "Beware of the 'can of peas' shopping." What I meant by that was when couples were taking pictures of themselves picking up a can of peas at Kroger, it's probably not a good marriage because nobody takes pictures of themselves shopping for peas except for someone who's trying to prove the marriage thing.

The Nigerian lady sent in photos to prove her marriage. Interestingly enough, the newlyweds had photographed themselves at a party. In one photograph they sent in, you could see the Nigerian lady standing next to the guy from Ghana. They're right next to each other. The Nigerian lady has a child. On the other side of the woman is another man. I do not know who he was. Then, you guessed it, on the other side of that male is the homeless man officially married to the Nigerian lady. Don't photobomb your U.S. Immigration photos with all of the fraud participants.

Now, in the process of getting close to the Nigerian lady's circle of friends and zeroing in on the targets in the investigation, she got wind that I was doing an investigation on her, which is not uncommon. When a U.S. immigration officer starts knocking on people's doors, and you've been in the same place a long time, people know, including lawyers. Your face becomes familiar.

One of the dirty tricks that people use when you are getting close to the suspect, and they know they're going to get in trouble and most likely get caught, is filing an application under VAWA (Violence Against Women Act). This also can be filed by men, too. The form is an I-360 application for a battered spouse. This is exactly what the Nigerian lady filed, knowing there was no way we could ever prove the homeless guy did not abuse the Nigerian lady, let alone find him in the first place. The marriage fraud immigrants know every trick in the book, and this is the dirtiest one because it undermines the legitimate efforts to help women in abused relationships, including clogging up the system that supports battered women.

I got wind that she had filed an I-360 as a battered spouse. I reached out regarding this case to the Vermont Service Center, where everyone files. Vermont Service Center is the U.S. immigration hub for Mid-Atlantic and Northeastern states. I sent all the records up to them, all the information. We do a summary of findings and write up a report. I outlined everything. I had all the images in there, I had all the information from each one of these places explaining what was going on, explaining the intricacies of the relationships, and how it all fits together. Explained the fact that the guy from Ghana and the U.S. citizen from Alabama were never found together. I further explained the Nigerian lady actually lived with the guy from Ghana, and they had a baby together. I documented that they never lived at the house with Mom and that they never lived in the senior living center. The pictures explained the fact that she had used three different names to try to enter the country and did all that fraud in the U.S.-Nigerian visa offices.

Vermont Service Center is notorious for approving these VAWA cases, and there is another story about that as well. They will approve almost all of them. The exception is it's more likely that if you're a male and you file for a battered spouse, you'll be denied more than the women. They will deny cases where the applicants do not respond to a request for evidence. But most approve beyond that. I would suspect more of the men who filed for the battered spouse are battered more than some of the women. There have been complaints raised about that in immigrant communities. Most of the filings I have seen come through my hands by men were denied.

Protecting battered women through the Violence Against Women Act (VAWA) is a top priority for the federal government, as it should be. However, like anything else in life, when there are rules to protect people, con artists will take advantage of the process. Unfortunately, the word is out, and the VAWA filings are seen as the Golden Ticket. They're almost untouchable. You can't dig too deep. You can't take the word of any family member of the so-called batterer. Your hands are so tied that certain dubious immigrants know it. Almost all evidence is off the table unless it is from unbiased observers. Well, that rarely exists. But in this case, I had a lot of information that showed that the Nigerian lady's case for VAWA was a total sham. And I presented it to Vermont, and they still approved this case. They approved the Nigerian lady's I-360, which is a direct pathway to U.S. citizenship. My investigation proved the fraud without a doubt, and they still dismissed my investigation.

They don't even know to whom they granted this battered spouse status because she had three different names and three different identities. I used to say that was the reason to deny anything or anyone. I don't know what's happening at the Vermont Service Center; their bar is low. Evidence and reality matter nothing to Vermont. I'm frustrated with the process, especially since it takes away time and energy from the women who actually need the protection.

VAWA Fraud

The immigrant wives would file police reports against homeless African-American men as battered. These men had no homes. They didn't live anywhere. They often didn't know initially that there was a report out on them, let alone a police report on them being abusive. Often, these women would use those reports to go and get a restraining order against the gentleman they claimed to be married to. I don't know if it was out of a sense of guilt or strategy, but they would often go back later on and get those restraining orders rescinded. Usually, after they receive their permanent residence (green card).

Now, I understand people in real relationships do this all the time. I'm not naive. I've been around a long time. However, the cases I dealt with were not real relationships. I'll go even further ... None of the VAWA cases I dealt with were real relationships. None of them. The homeless guys were preyed upon by a syndicated network of marriage arrangers, immigrants, and handlers.

Shockingly, some immigrant scammers even went down a more sadistic path. These immigrant women involved in the fraud would have people beat them up and punch them in the face. They'd have their real husband or a friend do it to them voluntarily and then take photos for the police. This was so they could prove that somebody beat them up. I heard confessions of this sick technique from people who would do this— insane! I had other people send in signed letters, or I interviewed them, and they explained how this method was done.

This self-harm or mutilation was immortalized in a Clint Eastwood movie where the psycho murderer hired a guy to beat him severely in the face to pin the assault on *Dirty Harry* (the namesake detective in the 1971 movie). The psycho killer paid cash to the professor-looking thug/enforcer, who then mused, "You really want $200 worth (of beating)."

The psycho killer responded, "Every penny of it."

These are the moments as an American, a U.S. immigration officer, and a human being that make you reflect, "What the hell is going on in this life? Is the rest of the world so horrible that people will get the *Dirty Harry* $200 beating to manipulate the system? Have we all gone mad? Does our dysfunctional system manifest this environment? Should I have been an accountant? Somewhere in a lonely room is a woman who actually got beaten by an abusive spouse. What would she think of this manipulation of the VAWA program? No wonder people think we should let everyone into the country, or should we severely tighten our belt?"

Many of the VAWA women who claimed to be battered would go and see a psychologist. They would go to some counseling program to get a note or a necessary paperwork trail. The majority of the time, they would go and see a counselor one time. They would talk about the buzzwords and use the right lingo when they were talking to the psychologist to get that psychologist to write a letter saying, yes, this person suffered from PTSD (post-traumatic stress disorder).

Hey, they went to see a counselor. Counselor says they have PTSD from the battery, but anyone could fake that in one visit. Anyone can look up the symptoms and effects of battery. Then use the right lingo or act a certain way. For one visit anyway. They can say, "I'm feeling bad."

And the counselor would say, "The victim came into my office. She said that her husband beat her up. She said she was suffering from night sweats or claimed she was scared to go outside, to eat."

The counselor would then write her up as a battered spouse.

Why all of this? Always know that a green card is an extremely valuable thing. People have killed U.S. citizens to obtain a green card. Again, immortalized in the movie *Scarface* when Tony Montana said, "...

For a green card, I'm going to carve him up real nice." As disturbing as it sounds, some immigrant women have let someone punch them in the face to get a VAWA-induced green card.

I know many of you won't believe this and won't accept it; however, twenty years of service as a U.S. immigration officer showed me otherwise. The Kenyan nurse case, unfortunately is not uncommon.

Long-distance VAWA

The Violence Against Women Act (VAWA) impacted my agency, USCIS (United States Citizenship and Immigration Services), in many ways. VAWA allows a strong pathway to help women and even men who were sexually assaulted or battered. Unfortunately, VAWA's protective powers are taken advantage of by fraudsters. It's difficult for me to even fathom misuse of VAWA since I was taught from an early age to believe in all women. As a fraud officer, I am taught to be skeptical. The conflict between believing all women and being skeptical of fraudsters abusing the system weighed heavily on me.

The stories I'm about to tell could be repeated in different forms. There are little nuances to each of them, but all have the same pattern. When I first started with U.S. Immigration, the perception was that women were coming into this country and being abused. The stereotype that was used was an average white man beating up a beautiful Eastern European immigrant woman. That was the image that was pressed on us in our training.

When I first started working for USCIS, I will let the truth be known: I saw a lot of Russian and Eastern European women who were filing for VAWA. You could hear some pretty horrific stories about these women being abused. However, when you were in the office looking into it, you could tell that a lot of these were shams. You couldn't necessarily prove it, but you had some really deep suspicions about them. There were a lot of men whose lives were ruined by these accusations.

U.S. Immigration ended up doing research on VAWA. Any female immigrant could access online immigration websites and find people discussing how to file for VAWA and how to use it to get a green card or citizenship. Essentially, they figured out how to manipulate the system and accused husbands of serious crimes.

Shockingly, we would get audio tapes, text messages, and emails, hard evidence from the husbands who were accused by their immigrant wives. The immigrant wives were so brazen they would threaten to use VAWA as a leverage tool against their husbands. Essentially, they were admitting there was no abuse at all, but VAWA was a valuable bargaining chip. Of course, we weren't allowed to use any of that stuff because it came from the husband, the "batterer." Under the strict rules of VAWA, even though there was hard proof, all the evidence was inadmissible to defend the husband or stop the fraud.

Don't get me wrong. There were some serious abuse cases. I've certainly seen frightened women who needed VAWA, and it was a blessing. I always took this seriously. I have experience with battered women. My father battered my mother. I have images from my childhood of that going on in my head and nightmares. I know abusive relationships. I can understand them. So, I'm not insensitive to this, and I am protective of the woman who needs VAWA.

I do, however, want to give you an idea of how VAWA is abused. I want you to remember the magnitude of the fraud.

This story involves a lady in her early twenties who came from Kenya to attend nursing school in Atlanta under a student visa. She graduated from the university and became a nurse. That's the true part of this story.

She entered the country in June. The next month, the Kenyan nurse went to Los Angeles to visit a friend before starting classes. While she was in Los Angeles, her friend introduced her to a gentleman who was living there. This was an African-American gentleman, older than the Kenyan nurse. He was in his early to mid-thirties when they met. According to the Kenyan nurse, they immediately fell in love. They ended up getting married in Los Angeles in August of that year. So, within a month of meeting and three months of entering the United States, the Kenyan nurse was married to a U.S. citizen. She claimed that her newlywed husband's family owned a business in Los Angeles, so he had to stay in Los Angeles for some time while the Kenyan nurse came back to Atlanta to begin university.

The Kenyan nurse's husband was going to come out and live with her in September after he got his affairs in order. She claimed her husband flew to Atlanta a month later, in September, to start living together in matrimony.

She then claimed that within the first week or two of them living together, her husband began to abuse her. She called the police and made a police report on his abusive behavior, saying that he hit her and slapped her around. The Kenyan nurse claimed to the police that he even took her red car and drove off. The next thing she knew, he was back in Los Angeles.

Looking through her police reports, they never contacted the husband and never were able to arrest or interview him. However, the fact she filed a report was enough for filing the I-360 visa application for a battered spouse with U.S. Immigration. This seemed an excellent case to invoke VAWA. Further evidence showed the Kenyan nurse next filed a protection order request with the courts, referred to professionally as a PFA (protection from abuse) commonly known as a restraining order. This is all standard practice, right? The system was working in a good way. Once the Kenyan nurse had all this paperwork together, she filed the I-360 visa petition for a green card. Oddly, the Kenyan nurse went back to the local criminal court and withdrew her request for a restraining order.

Just so you understand, this is all either the Kenyan nurse's testimony or some of the records that she submitted from the local police or criminal courts. She also filed information with USCIS, such as letters from friends, acquaintances, and other people, witnesses to the abuse that she experienced from her USC spouse for over a year. One such letter described events that occurred on February 14th, seven months after the marriage. In the letter, a guest at the Kenyan nurse and husband's Valentine's party described a violent incident. The Kenyan Nurse had made a pie for the USC husband to show her love for him on Valentine's Day; nothing says love like a chocolate pie.

The guest claimed the USC spouse was a little drunk and angry with him for flirting with his Kenyan wife. The Kenyan nurse's husband became angry, slapped the pie out of her hand, and shoved her to the ground. She was consoled by the guest who observed the whole event.

The next claimed event was in April. The couple got into an argument because he wasn't working. He couldn't find a job in Atlanta. The Kenyan nurse felt like she was carrying the whole load, so they got into an argument. He got mad at her again, slapped her around, and busted her lip, then shoved her out the door and told his Kenyan nurse wife he didn't need her in the house ... Get out! Coincidently, the same guest from the Valentine's Day party also happens to be the witness in the busted lip crime.

The third story the Kenyan nurse told was about an event in May. She had gotten back together with her husband, and they were at a Memorial Day party with some friends. Her USC spouse again accused her of flirting with the same original guest from the Valentine's Day party. Seems like they shouldn't have kept inviting this attractive and magnetic male guest. The USC spouse was jealous. He ended up pushing the Kenyan nurse down on the ground and punching her in the head. Again, this was the same original guest who supported her story the other two times.

Now, all of these things seemed fairly plausible, right? I can understand that happening. I can see someone being jealous and angry. You get these stories all the time. You've probably seen stories where boyfriends and girlfriends are jealous of each other, get angry, and yell and scream at each other. Maybe someone gets pushed around or even worse beaten.

As I've told you many times, USCIS and FDNS (Fraud Detection and National Security), in particular, can do a lot of background checks on people. They're all kinds of systems that exist. There are systems where we can check and see who is coming in and out of the country. How often do they travel in and out of the country? Who might they be traveling with? CBP (Customs and Border Protection) have database systems that USCIS can access. USCIS could not check to see who was traveling domestically, only internationally travel. I could not tell who flew from Los Angeles to

New York or from Houston to Minneapolis. We never check those. We don't even have access to a system that allows that.

We have systems that allow us to check people's criminal backgrounds. We could pull up criminal records for people when they've been arrested, if they've gone to jail, and how many times they've been convicted of a crime. The system tells us what occurred. To get more details, we have to reach out to any court or jurisdiction that may have more information about it, and that's usually the clerks of the courts, the jails, the prisons, and local law enforcement. We can request information from those sites and get full details of any documented event. We usually do this by asking the applicant if they have a criminal background and to give us the information. U.S. Immigration can go directly to the source to verify and further investigate.

I'm going to tell you the other side of the Kenyan nurse story, the other side of the coin. I did research on the Kenyan nurse's VAWA case. I found out that the U.S. citizen's husband had a long criminal history. Her U.S. citizen spouse had spent a lot of time in jail or prison.

Normally, this might bolster the whole idea that he was a batterer. He was a mess. He had a criminal past. Mind you, he had no record of violence. In this VAWA case, he was certainly accused of violence. The husband had an extensive drug history and an extensive arrest record for car theft, breaking into cars, stealing, and vagrancy. All kinds of issues. That seems like a real problem. But no violence to another human being in any of those arrests.

The problem stems from the fact that all of his arrests were in Los Angeles, especially related to the Valentine's Day incident. The problem with the Valentine's Day story was the husband had been arrested in December, about two months before he was supposedly beating his Kenyan nurse wife. The husband had been arrested for several instances and was still sitting in a Los Angeles County jail on February 14th when he was supposed to be abusing his wife in Atlanta, Georgia. That's what's called a solid alibi.

I researched further into the second domestic abuse incident in April when the husband allegedly beat his Kenyan wife. The husband was actually in prison in California during this time. I was able to get a record of his time in jail and his time in prison from both the county and the prison itself. Each incarceration record showed he was there, checked present on daily roll calls, and the Kenyan wife never went to visit him. Of all the quick prison releases you see on TV in Los Angeles, the husband wasn't so lucky, or maybe there was a silver lining since the prison records cleared his name in the VAWA case with his wife.

At some point, he got out of prison quickly. In May, the husband was arrested again for breaking into cars and for having stolen a car. He was sitting in a Los Angeles County jail for grand theft auto, awaiting trial for that arrest. At the same time in May, the husband was supposed to be battering his Kenyan nurse wife. In all three major domestic violence incidences, the accused husband/batterer had airtight alibis.

The husband was in prison in June of that same year. He was in prison for six months after another car conviction. I did not get the court documents related to that. I only obtained the prison and county records of him being incarcerated, which showed he was obviously innocent of any battery on this woman. What I can tell you categorically is the evidence showed that the husband was nowhere near Atlanta during the times his Kenyan Wife claimed to have been beaten, battered, mistreated, and harmed.

The second focus of my research on the Kenyan Wife VAWA case revealed critical information about the ever-present witness or coincidental witness to all three spousal abuse filings with the police. As you remember, I referenced being able to search a database of people coming and going out of our country. I had a good idea that something was off with the frequent guests of the parties who always witnessed the U.S. citizen (USC) spouse beating, harassing, and abusing the Kenyan nurse. Well, when you looked at the records for her travel, I could see that she took a few cruises to the Bahamas, and the frequent guest, Johnny on the spot witness, had traveled with her on every one of those trips. During that time, she was still married to her USC spouse.

This woman had been granted battered spouse status. You may ask how. The officers in Vermont have the same ability as I do. They could have easily reviewed the criminal record of the husband. Saw that the whole time he was supposedly abusing her, he was thousands of miles away. The short answer is that Vermont does not look too deeply into these cases. Now, they will tell you they deny a lot of VAWA cases. But those cases are for the applicants who do not respond to requests for information. They really do not dig deep enough into these cases. Furthermore, how does a person in Vermont really investigate a fraudulent VAWA case in Colorado? The short answer is they don't. She was granted legal permanent residence based on the battered spouse status, not the student visa, which is less powerful. In fact, the Kenyan nurse had been in front of a U.S. immigration officer in Atlanta applying to gain U.S. citizenship (above green card status) based on her claimed abuse by her USC spouse. Essentially, the Kenyan nurse wife was accusing her imprisoned U.S. citizen husband of abuse, and from that, she was going to be a USC.

I want you to understand this is not an isolated incident. I saw this repeatedly with Vermont. This African-American gentleman had some drug issues. He had some criminal issues. He was down on his luck. He had some problems. The immigrant nurse took advantage of his plight. This is usually done with a network of marriage arrangers and handlers. Even the Kenyan nurse most likely knew the discrepancy in the timeline of events was going to be exposed. She must have known her spouse had a criminal record because she must have communicated with him during that period.

The U.S. citizen spouse was truly destitute from examining his records and police reports and reading through his profile.

When I talk about most of my VAWA cases, the Kenyan nurse case epitomizes the fraud template. Out of all of the cases that I dealt with in all my years, I will tell you the overwhelming majority of them were like the Kenyan nurse and the U.S. citizen in Los Angeles marriage. They were bogus BS. Most of them targeted were African-American men. Most often, homeless people have drug issues. People who didn't have a steady home or steady job. People already dealing with mental health issues are marginalized people. People who are hard to find, people who were down at the bottom, easy to take of advantage of, easy to disappear, and hard to find.

Dekalb County "Courthouse Steps"

My first large marriage fraud courthouse case was out of Coweta County. This led me to look at more countries. I began to wonder how this was working in other places. Could I find a template or repeated pattern? How are so many people getting married? How many people are engaged to undocumented immigrants, and how are they meeting? There's a lot involved in marriage fraud, a spider's labyrinth, but will the fraudulent marriage arrangers get dangled or caught in their own deceit?

I'll unpack some of that for you as we go along with the DeKalb County cases. But first, a little more background. One of our jobs as immigration officers is to be a liaison. We are supposed to reach out and work with other federal agencies, other organizations, and departments at the state and county level. A larger range of communication with everyone might help us do our job better. No one that I knew at the federal level branched out for information, coordination, and communication. When I first started at U.S. Immigration as an FDNS officer (Fraud Detection and National Security), I compiled a list of all the people I was in contact with in the different welfare systems: government housing individuals and other federal agencies that we normally don't work with, Social Security, HUD (Housing and Urban Development), and local state agencies. I thought this network might be of assistance to solve problems. I compiled a nice list of individuals at the local level and at the upper levels of state government that I could work with. And I made this list available to every officer in FDNS Atlanta. I hoped that everybody would contribute. We would have a nice list of all the contacts we needed, especially people who were helpful to me. Also, I went to every courthouse around Atlanta and talked to the clerks of their courts. I went to Gwinnett County, Cobb County, Douglas County, Spalding County, and DeKalb County for starters.

I explained to them some of the things that I thought might be going on and what they might see. I asked some questions like, "Do you ever see people coming in to get married who maybe look like they have an arranger (fraudulent marriage matchmaker) or a handler (henchmen to the arranger who walks people through the courthouses)?"

Resoundingly, the answer always came back as, "Yes!" "Do you ever see that same handler come in?"

Again, "Yes!" Some were enthusiastic for us to be there, especially DeKalb County staff, who were helpful. I was able to get enough information to create my case. I obtained video evidence of the marriages. A lot of good information came from reaching out.

DeKalb explained that the handlers were in their courthouse all the time. I gave my email address to the clerks and officials and all my information on how to contact me. I asked the clerks if they saw any more of the third-party arrangers and handlers to please immediately contact me via email with copies of their suspicious applications.

Almost immediately, I began to get emails from the clerks for these types of cases where the individuals were coming in with arrangers and handlers to facilitate the marriage of immigrants to U.S. citizens. In two and a half years, the DeKalb County clerks provided me with 1,300 potential marriage fraud cases. I ended up creating a spreadsheet for all of these cases, and I'd put the names of the people who got married and the addresses where they claim to reside. Additionally, I noted what countries the foreigners emigrated from. This allowed me to sort these fraudulent marriages by country and what U.S. state and county they focused on getting married in.

What I ended up finding out was a definitive pattern to the multiple arranged marriages occurring in Atlanta from my database of different nationalities. I'm going to talk about these and pattern recognition as we go along.

Just to give you an idea of the multitude of different marriage fraud cases that were going on, there was one Jamaican case with a large fraud ring. I'll talk about an Indian case where there was an African arranger who was bringing in people to marry predominantly young African-American girls with Indian males for marriage. There were five different African fraud rings going on, with different arrangers sending their handlers to the courthouses to walk the immigrants through the process.

The first time I went to talk to the clerk of the court in DeKalb County Courthouse, I noticed something unusual when I was coming up to the court steps: four people, three men and a woman were leaving the courthouse. I've done so many marriage cases and so much fraud that they immediately stood out to me. The four were talking and laughing, and clearly, an event had occurred; I suspected at least a marriage. One of the men looked a little disheveled. I would describe him as a tall African-American male with a thin, scraggly face that had not been shaved in a while. His clothes did not fit well and were pretty old. I observed them coming out the door as I was getting ready to go in. I walked over to the corner of the front of the courthouse and stood there and observed.

I noticed that the one gentleman who was a younger guy kind of matched with the woman in the way she looked in appearance; better dressed in their mid to late thirties. I could hear them speak. They were both African; the older gentleman, probably homeless, was a little disheveled and spoke with a southern accent. The four were talking about the wedding that had occurred. Another gentleman who was there was kind of quiet. He had his phone out, taking pictures. Could the fourth person be the handler? He took pictures of the older man and the African woman in their happy moment. They chatted. I couldn't hear everything they said, and I really wanted to hear the full extent of the conversation. When the possible handler finished taking some photos of the presumed newlyweds, The well-dressed younger African man and the African woman hugged, turned, and walked away, arm in arm as a couple. The African-American man whom she had taken pictures with turned and walked away with the handler in the opposite direction.

I sat and observed for a while. I waited and wondered what they were going to do next; all four turned their respective corners and were gone. This wasn't my first rodeo, I'd done this for a long time, and I was familiar with it. That was most definitely an arranged marriage. The handler was the fourth of the party of four, guiding the fraudulent marriage couple through the process and documenting the event with photos for possible interviews with U.S. Immigration.

I walked through the DeKalb Courthouse and checked in. I then went down to the basement, where the people went to get their marriage certificates and talked to the clerk of the court, and that's when we had our discussion about all the marriages.

While I was there, I observed some people coming in who clearly looked like they were with a marriage arranger or a handler. It was clear to me that the DeKalb County Courthouse had been turned into a fraudulent marriage factory combining financially desperate U.S. citizens with immigrants looking for citizenship. The clerk of the court gave me a copy of some marriages that she spotted as arranged. She'd been stacking up a large file. The clerk of the court stated that she had been saving them because she thought something was wrong and that perhaps one day, she would have someone to give them to. I thanked her for being responsible and insightful.

The next day, I brought another U.S. immigration officer with me due to the sheer volume, and we went back to talk to the clerk of the court. We were looking for more information to figure out the extent of the marriage fraud networks. Also, I went to see the DeKalb sheriff to see if I could get some video of the first group of four outside of the courthouse, as well as to get some videos of others I saw while in the clerk's office. Hopefully, I could get images of them leaving in cars to run their plates or any other clues.

While I was waiting, I saw four to five couples come in. Each couple had someone assisting them in obtaining marriage licenses. These appeared to be arranged marriages. It was a well-organized and fluid operation.

And you may ask, how did I know if marriages were arranged? They were marriages that were occurring with handlers assisting them in the walk-through. The handlers weren't working for the county, they were working for marriage fraud arrangers. As the couples walked in the door, there was an individual with each of the couples coming to obtain a marriage license. In one instance, an African-American woman (a handler) was bringing in an Indian male and a young African-American female. In three hours, I saw four or five marriages fitting the classic marriage fraud profile. They appeared lost and uncertain of the strangers they were about to marry in a county courthouse. Some of the marriage fraud participants had to ask each other their names as they filled out the paperwork. In one instance, I watched an arranger bring a couple in, walk the supposed newlyweds through the process, and finally get a marriage license. Then, the arranger and newlyweds stood in front of the door, which had a security camera. The potential husband began counting out five one-hundred-dollar bills and paid the marriage arranger in cold hard cash. This was right at the entrance door of the courthouse in front of the camera—talk about brazen!

Love and Waffle House

When I first started, I named my overall investigation "Operation: Courthouse Steps." I had already interview a number of couples. One theme that came up often was how they had met at Waffle House. I went to the courthouse and interviewed people, one of the things I learned was that multiple arrangers were setting up shop in the courthouse, all marriage fraud kingpins.

When I went to the DeKalb County Courthouse, I noticed a Waffle House across the street from the courthouse, right in front of the main entrance of the courthouse. This was an "Aha" moment for me. I kind of got big and bulgy-eyed, and I started going, "Oh my God, there it is."

From then on, when I would interview people and I would talk to them about how they met in the Waffle House, it was a major clue marriage arrangers groomed them, and they eventually started confessing to me. In my field research surrounding Waffle House, I think I gained ten pounds, but at least I was happy. Many times, the fraudsters' confessions started with the first time they met their new African husband or wife at the Waffle House. So many U.S. citizens being paid for the fraudulent marriage would explain that the first time they met their arranged spouse was at the Waffle House. The U.S. citizen and immigrant spouse would sit there and have breakfast, wait for the court to open, talk for a few minutes, and go in and get their marriage licenses. Then they'd go upstairs in the court hours and marry. The irony was overwhelming: fast marriage license, fast wedding with a justice of the peace, and fast food (even though Waffle House cooks to order). DeKalb eventually changed the way they did their marriages. You could go get your license, then you could go upstairs, and a judge would marry the couple. DeKalb ended up processing so many marriages that they opened up an extra building to do marriages day and night. Who knew DeKalb was the new Las Vegas of the South in terms of weddings and hashbrowns?

Africans flying directly into Atlanta from their home country would be driven directly to the Waffle House. One immigrant who paid for his fraudulent marriage was dropped off by the arranger in front of the famous hashbrown place. The U.S. citizen is there. They had breakfast, they got married, and then the arranger got the immigrant a place to stay.

Marriage Salesman

This Story is part of the "Courthouse Steps" case, about some of the methods that marriage scammers called arrangers and their henchmen used in Operation: Courthouse Steps, and also some of the interesting things that I heard from immigrants and witnesses.

We talked to a lot of people who were getting married in Dekalb County, Georgia. When I say a lot, I'm talking about more than a thousand couples! I interviewed U.S. citizens who had gotten involved in the marriages, and those Americans are referred to as petitioners in the U.S. Immigration system … petitioning for an immigrant to be granted a green card or permanent residence. I interviewed immigrants who had married those Americans as well.

In Atlanta, immigration fraud is absolutely rampant. There are so many different groups of people involved in marriage fraud. There are multiple syndicates from all parts of the world. It's so widespread. On the DHS, DOJ, and INS side of the equation, it may be worse than the marriage fraud arrangers from the various international syndicates. Here's why: The immigrants themselves know that even if they get caught, they're not going to be arrested, they're not going to be convicted, and they're not going to be deported. Combine this systemic failure with the networks of arrangers, and you've got a larger flood of immigrants than you ever see crossing the Rio Grande River in Texas.

I heard this from so many immigrants, at a certain level of arrogance within the scammer immigrant community. They'll look you in the face and tell you, "You're not going to do anything to us."

Immigrants asking the question, "Why are you bothering me? You know nothing is going to happen." They're pretty brazen. Talk about spiking the football (an American football colloquialism for letting your opponent know you've scored a touchdown against them).

These arrangers are people who are going out into the community and recruiting U.S. citizens to get involved in marriage fraud. Black Jesus was one of the more interesting names of the recruiters. I talked to countless people in the community. When I ask who recruited them, quite a few would say, "I don't know his name, but we all call him Black Jesus." The people I questioned let me know of a man in a robe going around asking people to commit marriage fraud, blessing them with $500 after they married an immigrant.

Arranging marriages is a lucrative endeavor. The arrangers need Americans to marry and immigrants to pay, so they employed recruiters on both ends of that equation. Black Jesus and his disciples and recruiters went to poor neighborhoods and rundown apartment buildings in South Georgia, Clayton County, and Coweta County, south of Atlanta, into these different poor neighborhoods. They would go door to door in the low-income communities and ask people if they would like to earn $500 by marrying an immigrant.

Some of the neighborhoods even had security guards to monitor activity coming in and out of the neighborhood. The security guards knew Black Jesus and what he was doing. He was a fixture. The recruiting and $500 miracles were all routine.

People engaged in the marriages said Black Jesus had long dreads. He was kind of a thin guy. He's charismatic. He reminded them of Jesus with his looks. I guess he was kind of hip and cool. He literally went door to door, randomly knocking to find new people. Black Jesus was a recruiter kingpin, accompanied by his compadres (marriage arrangers, recruiters, and henchmen). All in all, it was a big enterprise, racket, and syndicate, quite an involved and lucrative business.

I always had the image of a vacuum cleaner salesman who came knocking on your door. Young kids who would come to your door to sell you newspapers, magazines, encyclopedias, newspapers, and things like that. Perhaps Jehovah's Witnesses came to your door. But in South Atlanta, the people coming to your door are the disciples of Black Jesus devilishly tricking you into the underworld of fraudulent marriages.

U.S. citizens under Black Jesus's spell would often say that they had no idea who they were marrying, just that Black Jesus recruited them. He would take them to some place to meet the immigrant and the marriage arranger. Often, they would meet on the same day they married. The individuals would be brought to the courthouse by the handlers. The U.S. citizens would come with the recruiter, who were mainly other U.S. citizens themselves. The immigrant would come with the arranger, always a foreign national who may or may not have become a U.S. citizen, whether it was at the courthouse or a restaurant close by, usually the Waffle House near the Dekalb County courthouse. They would all immediately go directly to the courthouse after the first meeting. They would obtain a marriage license and most often marry on the same day. The U.S. citizen would get $500 for showing up for the marriage.

The U.S. Citizen would be promised another $500 to come to the immigration interview. Then, they were promised another $1,000 after the immigrant got their green card or permanent residence. Some U.S. citizens worked out agreements with Black Jesus or the people they married to get payments. Installment payments for $100 a month, $200 a month. Maybe the immigrant would pay their phone bill, something like that, or they'd transfer the money through Venmo, Cash app, or PayPal. Often, the money would be transferred to a friend's account. Then, Americans marrying the immigrant would get the cash from that friend.

I wasn't sure how deeply Black Jesus was involved in the marriage scene or if he truly was the kingpin. I knew for sure that he was one of several recruiters for the network or syndicate. But he was quite active, and I would assume if there was an employee of the month, he would win it a few times. Recruiters would get U.S. citizens involved.

Arrangers have a bigger role to play in this game. Arrangers always go to the courthouse and set up the immigration interview. The marriage arranger does all the other arrangements that need to be done and the paperwork that has to be filed. Often, the arranger did the taxes, obtained employment letters, and helped the couple get a lease, real or fake. That's why arrangers make more money from the more sophisticated level of paperwork and the ability to interact with and manipulate the county courthouse and federal systems.

Now you have to think, I caught 1,300 of these marriages. The U.S. citizen got $500. That's only what I caught. My rule of thumb is you catch 10% of the fraud that's going on. So the amount of money that exchanged hands from these 1,300 marriages where half of the relationship, or 650 American citizens, are receiving at the bottom level $325,000 or $3.25M if you count the fraudsters, I didn't stop. This was in the Atlanta area. That doesn't seem like a lot of money. In addition, each recruiter was making six figures a year tax-free.

The U.S. citizens got another $500 to attend the immigration interview, ring up another $325,000. The recruiter received $500 per marriage, adding up to another $325,000. The U.S. citizen was promised another $1,000 after the immigrant obtained legal permanent residence, costing $650,000. Payouts to the recruiter and American citizen total to a $1,625,000 payout.

On top of that, most immigrants told me that they had to pay between $6,000 and $10,000 to the arranger for each marriage, bringing the kingpin's total take up to $3.5M. A good profit margin for the top of the food chain.

Mind you, these numbers are for DeKalb County and only for the Nigerian cases I worked on. I do not even discuss here the number of marriages for SE Asians that are in the country. Those are a different set of arrangers. Further, African-American women often team up with men from India. Thousands of those marriages. East European marriage groups, not a lot of those, but still some. Latin American groups, Caribbean marriage arrangers. This became overwhelming.

The possible penalty for a U.S. citizen to get for entering into a marriage fraud is $250,000 fine and five years in prison; that's written on all the documents that you read. I don't know a U.S. citizen in Atlanta that's ever either been fined or imprisoned for it. One of the reasons that you don't find them is you need them to confess and to give you more information on someone else up the syndicate ladder. So they're never tried or convicted of any of this stuff.

You have to think I had over 120 Jamaican marriages that were not in DeKalb County. They were visiting from Albany, Georgia, plus hundreds of West Africans married U.S. citizens in Albany. So if you combined all the cases that I worked on. We are talking millions and millions of dollars in the three years that was investigating them.

Bear in mind that I never went to Fulton County, Georgia, the largest county in Atlanta. I was so swamped with the ones that I had I didn't see any reason to. I did go to Douglas County, Georgia, and was starting to receive a good bit of fraudulent marriages from Douglas County. But primarily, my marriage fraud cases, 2,500 that I did, came from four areas. The majority of them came from DeKalb County. The next group came from Cobb County, Georgia, Coweta County, Georgia, and also the city of Albany, Georgia. Just in those four areas, those areas alone gave me almost 2,500 fraudulent marriages. There were a ton more of them.

We couldn't get to all of them. The internal pressure to adjudicate and let everyone pass is so great that you're never going to finish them all. They're going to approve most of them.

I had always suspected that immigration fraud was much worse than the number Washington, DC, put out. I never imagined it was that rampant. You will often hear Washington say ten percent of marriages are fraudulent. That is not even close; they pull that out of thin air. It is much worse than ten percent. My guess is a minimum of thirty percent and as high as fifty percent of immigrant marriages are fraudulent.

Coweta County

One of the first big marriage fraud breaks that U.S. Immigration received was in Coweta County, Georgia, which ultimately led to the story "Operation Courthouse Steps" and Operation Marriage Hall (Cobb County cases). The Coweta information, evidence, and clues came from local law enforcement and hardworking public servants. Coweta County was investigating some issues with financial fraud, and simultaneously, the local clerk of the Coweta court was having an issue with an unusual amount of people coming in to get married. During Coweta's investigation, the detectives were able to link the two issues together.

They started collecting a lot of marriage applications, a lot of video and camera work, and information related to arrangers (fraudulent matchmakers) bringing in people to marry in Coweta County. Coweta County is a suburb of Atlanta to the south. It's a relatively small but growing community. Generally, it's not a hotbed of immigration or even any kind of issues with immigration. The clerk started noticing that a woman was bringing in people pretty regularly to get married, the same woman with all different types of people—your classic description of an arranger.

In the course of the investigation, I think I ended up with 100-plus marriage fraud cases. How did this little town end up being a marriage mill? It was all thanks to one family and the matriarch of that family. We were able to get a videotape. We had pictures of all of her arranged marriages. The police had done surveillance. Again, there's a lot of information related to this case from local law enforcement, who really did thankless grunt work to gather the evidence.

The main arranger was an African American woman from Coweta County in her fifties who was a chief recruiter of U.S. citizens to fraudulently marry immigrants. The arranger was working in tandem with a man from Africa to get these marriages processed. The arranger married two different African men herself. So she understood the procedures and what needed to be done. Then, the same arranger had her sister marry an immigrant African man. After that, her daughter married an African man. And even her son married an African woman. Talk about keeping it all in the family.

She had a lot of people in her community, especially people in financial distress, living in Section 8 housing with serious financial issues. I went to a lot of Section 8 housing areas. This is government-assisted living in poor and depressed areas. I had to track down these marriages and spent a lot of time in Section 8 to find the people involved.

The arranger organized tax records, leases, and insurance to show a valid marriage. She assisted one woman who married her son in the filing of a Violence Against Women Act (VAWA) application. My understanding was that her son wanted out of the scheme. So, the arranger/mom helped concoct the story that he was violent. Thanks, Mom. This arranger was pretty ruthless. The Coweta arranger expanded her family involvement to include nieces, nephews, and anyone who attended a family picnic.

And this is one of those cases where you say, well, you know, what's the big deal? It's marriage, and unfortunately, the U.S. Assistant District Attorney felt the same way. But as mentioned, marriage fraud is a gateway or stepping stone to larger crime. In for a penny, in for a pound. The arranger worked in the insurance industry and cultivated fraudulent tax returns. It was a big family affair and lucrative for the familial arranger. I found that the arranger had been doing this for over 20 years, dating back to the 1990s. I was convinced the number of cases that U.S. Immigration linked to the arranger was the tip of the iceberg.

Of course, the next phase for the arrangers is teaching new people the trade; let's expand the operation. We know we're not going to get prosecuted by ideologues in the Federal system; let's build a marriage fraud Empire, ala Tony Montana in the movie *Scarface*. Just for a little salt in the wound, the arrangers, even if they got caught, were arrogant enough to tell you that they're not going to be in trouble for this. Why are you bothering me? I heard that quite often from arrangers and their henchmen handlers. Even they understood they would not be prosecuted.

Meanwhile, boots on the ground at the local level, Coweta County, weren't happy with the brazen abuse of the county courthouse, and the whole scam reached a tipping point when Coweta put their foot down and started gathering serious empirical evidence. I can't praise Coweta enough because these cases are linked to other counties all over the State of Georgia and metro Atlanta. I talked to people at the local newspaper in Coweta County that was unwittingly suckered into some of the schemes. One man assisted in performing marriages outside the courthouse. Eventually, U.S. Immigration and the Coweta Clerks and Sheriff noticed a slowdown in the marriages because the arrangers started to get wind of our investigations.

I had thirty-five confessions from people who were involved in Coweta marriage fraud. Thirty-five people admitted that the Coweta arranger was the mastermind of the entire racket. They admitted the marriages were fraudulent, applications falsified, and supporting documents were bogus. Also, the thirty-five admitted they never lived with their faux spouses. Many of the Coweta arranger's family members turned on her and confessed.

The Coweta arranger was also hot and heavy into income tax fraud. The arranger was creating income taxes for the immigrants, and she would use other income tax firms: addresses, and phone numbers, and fake tax EID (Employer Identification Numbers) for the companies. The Coweta arranger actually submitted completed tax records for these immigrants using random accounting firm names. And how do I know that? I reached out to some of these accounting firms and asked those questions and showed the returns the Coweta arranger filed in their company name. They were in shock. The accounting firms knew none of these people the taxes were supposedly filed for.

Our multitalented arranger also did insurance sales. At one time, she had a small house in Coweta County. The house that she kept continued to be rooted in the neighborhood and was used as a base camp for marriage fraud.

The Coweta arranger expanded beyond her family and brought outside people into the racket. And it was lucrative. I projected her doing a consistent volume over twenty years. As I mentioned, I only dealt with about 100 marriages, but that was of the applications that were currently pending or currently available to me. That certainly doesn't count all the ones that she successfully got through. I projected that she could have easily done 1,000 fake marriages or for 20 years, with the network in full operation. The Coweta arranger charged anywhere from $2,000 to $3,000 per marriage fraud. That's at least a cool $2,000,000 (two million U.S. dollars) over her career.

The Coweta arranger's sister became a recruiter as well and was heavy into it. All of her sisters' children married immigrants; it must've been quite a party at the family reunion. Their nieces and nephews were married to immigrants. I mean, the entire extended family was involved in this fraud. There was a young girl in their family who went to work for the Atlanta airport. She did not work there long, as we saw her at the airport twice, and she then quit the job. I had several cases involving individuals in the Atlanta airport. Customs and Border Patrol for years had problems with smugglers working at the Atlanta airport.

Coweta arranger was the first case where we gathered all the information to identify a marriage kingpin. We gathered as much detail as we could and had a Homeland Security specialist working with me who bundled it all together. He created spreadsheets charting the fraud ring and linked all the fraudulent documents that we had to each of the filings. Documents included fake leases, fraudulent tax documents, and written and signed confessions. Anything we could gather that was good evidence, we organized and had a rock-solid case. U.S. Immigration, along with the special agent, presented the entire case in detail to the U.S. attorney's Office in Atlanta. The first time we presented the Coweta arranger case, they sat on it for a year. No one contacted us; no one told us anything. Then DOJ moved it to another U.S. attorney. The second U.S. attorney sat on it for another year. We continued to work on the case, still trying to get more evidence. They gave it to a third U.S. attorney. All in all, they sat on the case for three years. Finally, they gave it to a fourth U.S. attorney with whom we had some dialogue until we all realized we were being asked to go out and jump through a lot of hoops to get the same information again. After three years and starting our fourth U.S. attorney, it had become a little bit stale. So we freshened up the investigation, we went back, we found people, we re-interviewed them, we got the information, and we got the same stories as it always had been. In some cases, it was difficult to find some of the people we had found earlier because years had passed, right? But we did what we could, and we took it back to this U.S. attorney (#4). He sat on it for almost a year. We talked to him again, and then he asked us to go out again and try to get more information. And we did that. I got the obvious feeling the DOJ was waiting us out to the point where some of us would retire, and the case would fade away into the Sunset.

I actually did transfer from the U.S. Immigration Office. Moved out of Atlanta for some other issues that were going on with immigration. That's a story in itself. I was gone a year, and we still talked about the case with the agent who was working on it and some of the people in my office, but it made no movement as the clock ticked to year five. They were still jumping through hoops for this U.S. attorney. In every case that I've done with "Operation: Courthouse Steps," all of the people that I had been investigating, all the different arrangers' cases, and different people who were recruiters that I worked to get charges against were all funneled into this one U.S. attorney.

On television news, you see state prosecutors elected to office for major cities who are being accused of apathy and dereliction of duty. It's nice to see the people react with recalls and outrage to the dangers that create, unfortunately, I got an early taste of that prosecutorial misconduct (not discretion). Insert any theory you want on why anyone in their right mind would allow crime to run rampant and overtly ignore the law; any way you slice it, it's wrong by any standard.

But in the Coweta County case, the U.S. attorneys had everything to push the case to prosecution. The immigration agent that I worked for would eventually be assigned a new job. He closed the Coweta arranger case after five years.

One of the things I will tell you: this guy was a good agent, a really good guy. He would email this U.S. attorney pretty regularly and try to expedite the cases. He never heard from the U.S. attorney, and he never responded to emails. We couldn't get in touch with the DOJ to expedite.

At this point, you can guess the one email the DOJ finally responded to. The Homeland Security agent emailed them and said, "I think we are going to drop this case because we were both moving on. I don't think anyone else in the office can take it up." After years of a few topical responses to case updates, the DOJ responded back within five minutes to this email: "Great, thank you, we're going to close the case." We didn't know whether to laugh or cry at such a quick response.

U.S. Immigration would go weeks and months without hearing from the U.S. attorney. Beyond that, the U.S. attorney had asked him over and over again to drop the case.

Beyond the immigration marriage fraud, the Coweta arranger case had tons of financial fraud and all kinds of criminal aspects to the investigation. But the DOJ was not going to touch it in Atlanta, and they didn't.

Cobb County

I often talk about "Operation: Courthouse Steps" and DeKalb County, Georgia. These were the cases that were sent to me by the DeKalb County Court clerk. She suspected these of being arranged marriages and identified arrangers. This is not a reflection on DeKalb County employees or the residents. I had a lot of marriage fraud cases out of DeKalb County; it was most likely a convenient place for a lot of immigrants to go and get married.

I also had a lot of fraudulent marriages out of Cobb County, Georgia. A couple of issues that I ran into out of Cobb were a little different and interesting. I'll spell out some of the generic things to set the table.

DeKalb and Cobb County shared some of the marriage fraud cases and techniques. I visited the Cobb County Courthouse Clerk and listened to their observations of unusual marriage activity. A few days later, I spoke to DeKalb County's Courthouse clerk and got the same spiel. On a federal-to-state-interaction note, I show my credentials every time I show up to the county courthouses. Cobb County video records the marriages, which is a goldmine of information. The clerks in DeKalb County told me the same story as the video evidence in Cobb. The arrangers, or modern-day paid fraudulent immigration matchmakers, would bring people in to get married and help them go through the marriage process. DeKalb County allowed the handlers (the runners who walk the immigrant through the fraud process) and arrangers (the kingpin matchmakers) into the clerk's office, whereas Cobb County didn't. Cobb would throw them out, like a casino bouncer throws out a card counter, especially when the marriage arrangers showed their poker hands or faces too many times. After booting the arranger or the handlers (henchmen to the arrangers), Cobb would process the paperwork and marry the couple anyway. Both counties thought it was highly suspicious and didn't know what to do about it.

The Cobb County clerks were grateful for me to come by, and they ended up sending me a ton of fraudulent marriages that the arrangers masterminded. The arrangers and Handlers used the same MO (Modus Operandi or criminal methods) in every county around Atlanta. The Handlers and arrangers got wind that U.S. Immigration was looking into them, so they spread out all over the State to throw us off the scent. The arrangers and Handlers were going into Paulding County and Douglas County further out from the center of Fulton County in the Atlanta area because we were tracking them and made some busts.

Cobb County is a major county, and Gwinnett County is a major county. They all have a lot of marriage fraud going on, but they handle it differently, and they handle their marriage processes differently, and they both might not see it as clearly from the sheer volume of marriages. Additionally, courthouses manage the logistics of people coming and going in certain ways. Cobb and Gwinnett County clerks don't necessarily see who brings someone into the courthouse, making it more difficult to look out for sleazy handlers in the clerk's office. The cop or county sheriff's deputies would throw the handlers out if they could spot them in the crowd.

Cobb County had an interesting aspect to its marriage fraud problems. There was a set of immigration attorneys, all originally immigrants themselves, who worked really hard and fulfilled the American Dream by all becoming attorneys in Cobb County. Adding to the centralization, the immigrant attorney group all worked out of the same building. They all worked together at some point in time. Just when you thought you had an American success story, U.S. Immigration learned the American Dream attorneys were more of a nightmare. A lot of the Cobb County fraud was run through the American Dream attorneys, but they had one interesting attribute that I always thought was kind of strange. The American Dream attorneys openly got away with many types of fraud, and no one cared. They tested the limits or boundaries of immigration fraud, and the

American Dream attorneys quickly learned that they could get away with almost anything they wanted, especially by listing bogus timelines and dates for their immigrant clients.

In Georgia, when you marry and divorce, especially when you are trying to get divorced, a couple must be a resident of Georgia for six months before they can even file the paperwork for divorce. Now, this wasn't what I got from the American Dream attorneys who worked in Cobb County. It wasn't enough that you were here or that you had to wait for six months to get a divorce; it was that you couldn't file. Technically, by Georgia Law, you could not file for divorce unless you've been a resident of Georgia for six months.

One American Dream attorney quite often filed before the six-month mandatory residence period. We (U.S. Immigration) had a lot of these cases from his firm. Just as a hypothetical example, let's say an immigrant couple flew in on April 1. When they came into the country, he claimed that they were married with children and residents in their own country. They would land in this country, and within two weeks, they would have met with these attorneys from this group, and they would file for divorce. One attorney from the group would file for divorce for one, and another attorney from the group would file for the other. In the divorce process, the married immigrant couple would say on an affidavit stating they've been a resident of Georgia for six months. And every one of the American Dream attorney's clients would claim that they'd been a resident of Georgia for six months, even though they'd been here for two weeks.

I finally got so frustrated with this brazen misrepresentation and abuse of the system that I formulated a plan to put a stop to it. I called all parts of Cobb County's district attorney's office, and the court. Many scam artists will try to take advantage of federal versus state issues and slither in between the cracks of the boundaries of the jurisdiction. I asked the entire justice system of Cobb County for their legal interpretation of the six months required residency for divorce, referencing the scam artist arranger's math of six months equals two weeks. Can someone get a divorce before having lived here for six months and make the decision to file for divorce?

They said no that you had to be a resident for six months before filing the paperwork, even if you were married in another country.

On top of that, I interviewed one client of the American Dream attorneys, and I asked, "Um, why did you file? You've been here two weeks, not six months."

The attorney popped up and goes, "Hey, Officer Lee, I don't know. I do what they tell me, I do what, you know, my client says."

I asked his immigrant client about it, and he said, "No, the attorney told me to do this. He told me to say that I lived here for six months."

So clearly, the attorney was prompting them to do his fraudulent attestation.

My argument was always that none of these divorces were legitimate. There were tons of these cases. But our U.S. attorneys didn't fight it. No one else wanted to fight it. So, the American Dream attorneys and their clients got the green light to game the system; the divorce was signed, sealed, and delivered. Then, before the ink was dry, the immigrants were already married to a U.S. citizen, and the immigrant was almost guaranteed to become a naturalized U.S. citizen.

So, as far as I could tell, none of these divorces were legitimate. But U.S. Immigration is not going to do anything about it, the courts are not going to do anything about it, and no one is going to put any pressure on the U.S. district attorneys to prosecute them. You pick and choose your battles, right? But that was kind of unique. It was one of the things that I saw only in Cobb County, and only that group of attorneys egregiously ignored the law.

At this point, you may understandably think that the American Dream attorneys were off the hook, but since they have multiple different types of cases, I would soon circle back around to get them on something else.

I had a big investigation on a different subject involving one of the American Dream attorney's filings. This attorney entered into a fraudulent marriage to get his benefits, and we investigated him. His marriage was old. The immigrant married another immigrant woman in California. That marriage failed to benefit him. He married another U.S. citizen woman in another state to get his benefits. His real wife was here with him. They lived together, they had children together. While he was supposed to be married to a U.S. citizen. It was one of those cases where they came in together; they got divorced, married a couple of people, then turned around after he got his benefits and married his original wife. Then, the immigrant became an American Dream attorney, a sham, dirty attorney. The Homeland Security Investigator I worked with on this retired in the middle of the investigation, and he dropped the cases.

The two big issues that I had in Cobb County were handlers facilitating fraudulent Marriage from arrangers and the "Six months = Two weeks" dirty attorneys' scam. In every county, the court clerks were concerned. Unfortunately, no one else was. They saw what was going on. They were powerless. There are no state laws against this, for the most part, and as you've come to find out, there's little or no chance of the Federal U.S. DOJ getting involved. The DOJ wouldn't want to prosecute, and no one wants to stop it. So, the marriage factory mill is going on there right now, I guarantee you, in Cobb County, DeKalb County, Gwinnett County, and Fulton County ... no doubt about it.

For the most part, schemes and sham marriages are all the same throughout each one of these county offices. In Cobb County, the scamming American Dream attorneys' concentrated involvement set them apart from other counties. The belligerence by the American Dream attorneys and how quickly they got their immigrant clients divorced and remarried to U.S. citizens was the shocking part.

Box of Credit Cards

This is a fraudulent marriage story that took place at the Cobb County Courthouse. As is typical, our featured couple came to the United States together with their children. They were coming to Orlando, Florida, on vacation from Nigeria. We're going to Disney World! For some reason, like so many couples heading to see Mickey Mouse, they ended up in the state of Georgia. They landed in Atlanta and never saw Mickey, Minnie, Donald Duck, or even Pluto. Instead, they immediately divorced in Georgia.

Both ex-spouses found new loves within weeks, married, and began their immigration journey. Both married U.S. citizens and those Americans petitioned for the Disney World divorcees to start the immigration process. In the course of my investigation, the USCs and the foreign couple never lived together, respectively.

The faux Disney World travelers came to my attention when the clerk of Cobb County Court reached out to me regarding marriage arrangers bringing people to the courthouse for fraudulent marriages. I obtained the Disney World couple's suspicious marriage applications, and I put out a "Be on The Lookout" (BOLO) alert for any government entity that was involved in these types of marriages. That way, when a Disney World couple filed an I-130 and I-485 (U.S. Immigration Application), they would be flagged, and the files would be sent to Fraud Detection and National Security (FDNS). This is exactly what happened. The couples were interviewed, and the files were then sent to FDNS (my world) for an investigation.

Remember, in previous stories, I had detected over 1,300 of these suspicious marriages in one county courthouse. I started doing research on the faux Disney World immigrant vacationers, and in the process of investigation, the U.S. Postal Inspector reached out to me. This couple was being naughty and doing a bit of identity theft, using the postal system to run scams. As I've said many times, marriage fraud is the gateway to larger crimes or with the fake Disney World couple, the starting gate. "Mirror, Mirror on the wall, who takes the most credit cards of them all?"

A lot of the BOLOs I put out would lead to other law enforcement agencies reaching out to me. I spent a good deal of my time working with Treasury, FBI, IRS, local law enforcement, U.S. Postal Service, Social Security, the DEA (Drug Enforcement Agency), and the ATF (Alcohol, Tobacco, and Firearms). Most of these marriage fraud cases were also involved in banking fraud, gun smuggling, drugs, and prostitution. They pretty much run the whole gambit. Instead of the vacationers hanging out with Daffy Duck, they were more likely to hang out with the D.A.

So, in this case, the Nigerian gentleman who diverted his trip from Disney World was involved in some serious financial fraud. One of the things that certain Nigerian criminals do well is identity fraud, but their identity fraud is sometimes different than other groups. Most Nigerians are hardworking and productive immigrants, but there's a small criminal element that does specific and damaging crimes. Nigerian fraudsters have a network or syndicate of criminals back in their country who fake and obtain real Nigerian documents using the immigrant's photo. They obtain birth certificates, passports, and Nigerian driver's licenses, you name it. They obtain hundreds of them. That person in Nigeria will then ship them via mail to the US. Sometimes, these identity documents are interdicted or intercepted in London or when they first come to the US.

When they are found by the UK Government or the U.S. Government, they'll track the documents to the recipient, letting them pass on to catch the criminals in the act.

I did an investigation and determined that the faux Disney World marriages were bad, and I talked to other federal law enforcement agencies. Postal was doing a warrant search on the properties for fraud. FDNS accompanied the raid. This allowed us to determine whether or not the marriages were good. And see the potential financial fraud.

Two of my colleagues with FDNS went to the Nigerian male's house with other Law Enforcement Agents. Another FDNS IO (Investigative Officer) and I went to the Nigerian female's apartment with law enforcement officers.

As FDNS officers, we do not go into the home with other law enforcement when they are conducting searches. We hang back and wait to see if the subjects are there. Then we talk to them. We'll interview them either after the raid has occurred or sometimes while law enforcement is searching the house. We'll interview them outside of the home. In this case, the female that we were looking for was not home.

So they did the search, and FDNS hung back and watched. Law enforcement brought out garbage bags full of identity documents. She was not organized. It was bags of fraudulent identities: passports, driver's licenses, and different things of that nature. The Nigerian lady had stored them in the closet.

While this was going on, Law enforcement and my FDNS colleagues at the other home managed to interview the Nigerian male about his marriage to a U.S. citizen. Law enforcement went through his house, and they found boxes of credit cards. This man was organized with the shoe boxes of credit cards stacked vertically in long rows. They were neatly contained from one end to the other. Hundreds of them were in his closet. Later, it was found that these cards corresponded with the IDs that the Nigerian female had in her possession. In time, the gentleman was indicted for financial fraud. I left the office before the end result. I assume that he was eventually prosecuted for this. It was interesting that the Nigerian female was not prosecuted for the same act as the Nigerian male. She was basically let off scot-free or unindicted. I never heard if she finally made it to Disney World.

Albany, Georgia

Most of my immigration stories center around the Atlanta metropolitan area, the largest city near my U.S. Immigration Office. That's where most people live in Georgia. There are five million people or more in that area. So, a lot of what you're going to deal with is going to be around Atlanta.

But the fraud isn't confined to Atlanta. One area of significant immigration fraud outside of Atlanta is the city of Albany in Southern Georgia, seventy miles north of the Florida-Georgia Line (which is also the name of a popular country music group). The immigration fraud concentration includes not only Albany but the surrounding counties, from Albany to eight to five miles northwest, up to Columbus, Georgia. This area makes up an unsuspecting immigration fraud hotspot with a connection in Dekalb County Georgia, and Panama City, Florida.

A tremendous amount of marriage fraud occurs in the area. Albany has a university, which might be part of the reason for the hotbed. Colleges and universities have a lot of F-1 student visa holders. They come for school and look to stay by marrying a U.S. citizen. Some are legitimate, but most are not. They are not marrying fellow college students. Many do not even stay to attend college, as we learned in the "Belletrist" story. They just disappear. But that's another story for another day.

I went down to the Albany area because we saw a spike in fraudulent marriages. I visited the local courthouse there and talked to the judge and clerk of the courts. They did not confirm a lot of fraud but did recognize some patterns of U.S. citizens marrying foreigners. Mind you, most of the marriages were between Albany residents who drove up to DeKalb County (one of the major counties of Atlanta) to marry American citizens. The trip from Albany to DeKalb takes about three hours one way.

The primary groups in the Albany area emigrated from Nigeria and Jamaica. I had identified five different recruiters working in the area. There's a huge Jamaican fraud ring in the Atlanta area that stretches all the way down to Albany.

This was a bit of a different fraud ring, well organized and yet decentralized across a large area: the main arranger/facilitator/matchmaker, whom I'll call the marriage kingpin, was in DeKalb County. The U.S. citizen recruiter was in Albany, and the Jamaican immigrants looking to get married lived in Panama City, Florida (150 miles southwest of Albany). Learning this information extended the web of the immigration fraud ring.

I gathered a lot of files and information, went down to Albany, and did some interviews. There are two challenges with this case: You have jurisdictional issues. Should this case be handled in Albany, in Atlanta, or should this case be handled out of Panama City? This case could either be prosecuted in Montgomery, Alabama (the federal district court that covered the Panama City, Florida area), the federal middle district court for Georgia (covering Albany), or prosecuted in Atlanta, where the main marriage kingpin operated. What we had to look at was where the money first changed hands and when was the start of the actual process. Additionally, where were the U.S. citizens initially recruited and possibly paid? I prayed that we could do this out of the federal middle district court closer to Albany. The middle district attorneys may have been friendlier to the prosecution. I was certain the northern district of Georgia (big city Atlanta) would not prosecute because it's so politicized with ideologues' who look the other way to immigration fraud and just let everyone come into the country no matter what.

The other issue was the distance and how spread out everyone was. How were we going to find them, bring them to one spot to get details and information to prosecute? Remember, most U.S. citizens are poor, often destitute, and many times homeless. It is never easy finding them or keeping track of them.

Focusing on the last component of the fraud scheme, Jamaicans who wanted to marry for green card status lived in Panama City, Florida. This marriage fraud case centered around one apartment complex in Panama City. Panama City is not a big city, but there were a lot of Jamaican immigrant applications from this one apartment complex. The U.S. citizens entering these marriages were out of Albany. I was battling some difficult spatial and logistical issues with U.S. citizens recruiting other U.S. citizens in Albany directly working for the marriage kingpin out of DeKalb County and Atlanta. The Albany recruiter was getting people to enter marriages with Jamaican immigrants who were living in Panama City. The suspect would run a van down to Panama City, pick up the Jamaicans, and bring them to Albany to meet U.S. citizens. The Albany recruiter would then bring the Jamaicans and U.S. citizens up to DeKalb County in a van under the watchful eyes of the Atlanta ringleader, the marriage kingpin.

I found some interesting information about this fraud case. A Jamaican gentleman was the main character in this scheme, also known as the marriage kingpin. He was working out of DeKalb County. In the beginning, he would meet the couples in a hotel in the Atlanta area. The story goes that he would get a hotel suite. The Jamaican immigrants and U.S. citizens would be taken from the hotel to the DeKalb County Courthouse, where they would obtain a marriage license and get married on the same day. After the ceremony, the Jamaicans and U.S. citizens would come back to the hotel to prepare for the immigration process. Several couples would meet in the lobby of the hotel. They would all sit around and wait for another person who worked for the marriage kingpin to come down the elevator and escort them to his hotel room. They wait in the lobby for their turn to be called up to the marriage kingpin's hotel room. The couple would go to the room, and the immigrant would pay the kingpin. The marriage kingpin would then explain the process. They would take pictures together. Sometimes, pictures would be Christmas-themed, with a Christmas tree and fake gifts under the tree, and sometimes other holiday themes. If the immigrant did not have enough money, one of the marriage kingpin henchmen would escort them to an ATM nearby to get the funds. So, the story goes that his hotel room was a high-end suite. The marriage kingpin was banking so much money off of this he'd become accustomed to luxury. The marriage kingpin had a personal chef who was in the suite cooking for him and setting up everything, and you would go in and meet him as if he were a king, modern-day royalty. The Jamaican immigrant would have to bring $6,000 to $10,000 for the process. The marriage kingpin would give the U.S. citizen from Albany $500 bucks for the marriage. The U.S. citizen was promised payments throughout the process: $500 for the marriage, $500 to complete the paperwork and go to the immigration interview, and $1,000 when the immigrant obtains a green card. None of the U.S. citizens that I had ever spoken to get that last payment. It never came. The U.S. citizen scammers got scammed themselves.

Essentially, once the green card was issued, the marriage kingpin had no more use for the U.S. citizens involved in the scheme and stiffed them out of the last $1,000 payment. As the saying goes, there's no honor among thieves.

The marriage kingpin was a bigwig in the Jamaican community. The Jamaican marriage kingpin made enough money that he bought a house in DeKalb County near the DeKalb County Courthouse. This house was set up so that he could do everything as a one-stop shop. The marriage kingpin had a room set up for photographs to show the marriage evolving over time. Unfortunately, style points aren't counted in immigration fraud investigations. A female USC petitioner said you would go there, and you would take pictures, you would take Christmas pictures, or you would take some other photo depending on the desired holiday theme. She stated that in her case, they took Christmas photos in the middle of July. The marriage kingpin must have been a fan of the Hallmark Channel's Christmas in July movies.

On a more serious note, the big issue for Homeland Security Investigations is the illegal smuggling of guns and automatic weapons by Jamaicans. Not only were they entering fraudulent marriages, but some were also involved in illegal gun smuggling, smuggling drugs and other contraband.

I have not spoken about the U.S. citizen recruiter in Albany who was a henchman for the marriage kingpin. I got this story from a couple of people that this gentleman was a bad drug dealer. And not the small-fry drug dealer on the street corner. The recruiter was a serious drug dealer. One of the women that I talked to was quite afraid of him because there were rumors in the streets that the recruiter had killed a fifteen-year-old kid who had double-crossed him over some drugs and money. This was to send a message to others not to steal from him. No one was willing to come forward on it. I don't know if any of that's true. But she had no reason to tell me outside of the fact that I was dealing with her marriage fraud case. But she was afraid of him.

Immigration fraud is more lucrative to the arrangers and recruiters than drug dealing. It is certainly safer, as the Atlanta U.S. DOJ will not prosecute most of these cases, and there are no equivalent criminal charges at the state level. More than half of all marriages that I dealt with as a U.S. immigration officer were fraudulent or highly questionable. It is hard to get them prosecuted.

Chain Stores Used for Fraud

Three major stores played a prominent role in my immigration career. These stores were Kroger, Walmart, and Payless Shoes. I want to be clear when I say this. None of these stores were ever involved in any immigration fraud. People would claim some connection to Kroger, but the company was not involved in any way. Reciprocally, this is an important story for the three companies to learn what goes on with immigration fraud and how people ping their companies in their stories.

The three stores play a large role in the Atlanta community. So people are familiar with these stores. The fraudsters could use them as backdrops for some of the things that they needed to do to show that they were married or had jobs.

The first and most common theme related to all three of the major stores and my stories was that marriage applicants would all take pictures in one of these three stores. These photos were of fraudulent or suspect marriages. I've talked about the "can of peas," where essentially, fraudulent spouses went to a store and took a group photo centered on a can of peas. No one would do that in real life, and it's easy to tag as a contrived photo for attempted supporting evidence for an immigration status upgrade. You're more likely to do that if you were a hand model for the Price is Right game show.

In my work, I saw where people would go into Kroger or Walmart to do their pretend grocery shopping as a happy couple, to at least appear as if they were going grocery shopping together as husband and wife. For some reason, they love to get in and pick up a food item.

Of course, you always ask them who took the picture. You know, why did you go into Kroger and take pictures of buying cans of peas? Or they could be standing overproduce, pointing at the carrots. Crazy things that you would never think a married couple would do.

I've been married for twenty years. I've known lots of couples as friends. I've never seen a photo of them grocery shopping, pointing at peas, carrots, beans, or holding up a can of peas or some chicken legs. But for immigration, for some reason, that seems to be a good thing to do. I have seen couples online who took photos of a fancy meal they got from a chef. That's art; the can of peas, not so much.

The other thing with Kroger that I saw during the period of "Operation: Courthouse Steps" was several immigrants coming to me with employment letters to support their applications. The U.S. citizens would have letters claiming that they worked for Kroger. The letters were on a fake Kroger letterhead and logo.

It mimicked the actual Kroger letterhead. Repeatedly, I was sent a letter saying immigrants worked for a warehouse in South Atlanta on Kroger letterhead. Unfortunately for these applicants, the Atlanta USCIS (U.S. Citizenship and Immigration Services) office sits right across the street from the Kroger corporate regional office. I would walk these letters over to the regional office and show them to the people that worked actually worked for Kroger. The Kroger executives explained the warehouse in South Atlanta that Kroger used was not actually owned or operated by Kroger. It was a warehouse Kroger contracted with to manage supplies. No one at Kroger worked there. No one at the South Atlanta warehouse would ever use Kroger letterhead because they're a different company.

I suspect someone either worked at that warehouse at one time or might have even still worked there and thought that it was perfectly OK to use the Kroger name. When I saw those letters for Kroger, I pretty much knew that it was going to be a bogus employment letter and a bogus marriage. You still have to verify; you still had to prove every one of the letters was not from Kroger. I spent quite a bit of time walking across the street to Kroger and never got a coupon.

Kroger Meat Department Love

I did have one case where the U.S. citizen actually worked at Kroger. He was involved in marriage fraud. This was an African American man, about thirty years of age, and he had married an African woman. They lived in the Northeast area of Atlanta. It was out past the Stone Mountain area in northern Gwinnett County.

One of my fellow immigration officers and I decided to drive up to talk to him and his claimed spouse. We arrived at their home at 6:00 a.m. It was still dark. We had a lot of work to do that day, so I broke my rule, and we went ahead and rang the doorbell and knocked on the door early in the morning. An individual peeked out of the upstairs window and asked us who we were.

We both showed our credentials as required and explained to them that we were with U.S. Immigration. We told them who we were looking for and asked if we could speak to them. The individual said that neither of them were at home.

The next thing you normally do is call either the U.S. citizen or the immigrant applicant. So I called the U.S. citizen husband. He claimed that he was at work at Kroger. He stated that he had gone in early in the morning and left at 5:00 a.m.

I asked him where his spouse was.

He stated that she was at home because he had left her there when he went to work this morning.

I told him, "No, she's not home either. Do you know where she may have gone?"

He said he didn't know where she'd gone, but she was there when he left. That was certainly a plausible story.

I asked the U.S. citizen husband where he was. "Can you tell me where Kroger is located with the address?"

He provided the information. The Kroger was five minutes from home.

I thanked him and got off the phone.

I called his claimed spouse while we were driving to Kroger. She answered on the first ring. The immigrant wife said that she had left the house at 5:00 a.m. She claimed to be visiting a friend who had picked her up. The friend had just gotten out of the hospital, and she was going to help her while she was recuperating.

I asked the immigrant wife where her spouse was.

She said she wasn't sure. "He may have gone to work, but I left before he had woken up. He was still home when I left to go meet my friend."

I asked the immigrant's wife about her location and if we could stop by and see her. She stated that she was on the side of the road off Ashford-Dunwoody. Now, Ashford-Dunwoody is a pretty populated area. The immigrant wife was also with her own two children from another man before her marriage.

I asked her why she was sitting on the side of the road and if she was with someone who could help her. The immigrant wife claimed that her friend had to go somewhere else and dropped her off on the side of the road with her two kids.

I asked her to give me some markers or some information about the area she was in. I was a bit worried about a woman on the side of the road in the dark with two children. The immigrant wife claimed that she was dumped on the side of the road in Dunwoody, Georgia, which has a tremendous amount of traffic. She said there were no buildings around her. There was a big open field, and she was standing on the side of the road in the dark, waiting on her friend to come back. What are friends for?

It was 6:15 a.m. by this time, and I was confused as to why this woman was sitting on the side of the road with her two children. One of her children was an infant, six months old. Not the U.S. citizen's child.

Regardless, she didn't know where she was, and she couldn't tell me how to get to her, so I was kind of at a loss. Hopefully, as a reader, you understand that none of that was true. The immigrant wife was not on the side of the road, and no friend had dumped her off on the side of a busy freeway. No friend had gotten out of the hospital and was recuperating, and certainly did not dump her on the side of the road because the friend was in a hurry.

I thanked her, and we got off the phone with her because we were pulling up at Kroger, where her U.S. citizen husband had said he was working.

My partner and I got out. We went inside, and we asked for the manager. The night manager came to us. We explained who we were there to see.

The night manager said yes, the U.S. citizen husband does work here. He wasn't sure if he was at work that morning. But he told us that the gentleman worked in the meat department. He walked us back to the meat department. Of course, the questions start flying. "Is he in trouble? What did he do? Did he do something wrong?"

We don't want to get someone fired. In case there's nothing wrong, you don't want someone to get in trouble for their job. We explained that sometimes people file for immigration documents, and we're there to verify the information and ask a couple of questions. That's about the best you can do because you can't give the employer or anyone else a lot of information.

The night manager took us back to the meat department, and he asked the meat department manager if the U.S. citizen husband was on the job.

The meat department manager looked at a roster there and told us he was not due to work until the next day.

I asked, "Have you seen him? Is he around here anywhere?"

The meat department manager said no.

We thanked him and went outside. I called the U.S. citizen's husband again. I told him, "I went into Kroger, and you're not there."

The U.S. citizen husband had the nerve to tell me that he was in Kroger working and he was in the breakroom. We walked back into Kroger, went back to the meat department, and informed the same meat department manager that the U.S. citizen's husband claimed that he was in the breakroom. "Could you check and see if the U.S. citizen husband is in the breakroom and let him know that we're here to see him?"

The meat department manager was kind enough to go in and check the breakroom. He came back out and told us no, the U.S. citizen husband was not in the breakroom at all.

I called the U.S. citizen husband back again and told him that we had gone into Kroger. He's not in the breakroom; he's not anywhere in the area.

This time, he told me that he had to leave Kroger quickly and go to the doctor's office. He said he went out the back door. He was driving to the doctor's office. Mind you, this is maybe 6:45 a.m. But he says he has to go and drop off some special medical paperwork for his job at the doctor's office.

The U.S. citizen husband explains that the doctor's office is in downtown Atlanta, off of North Druid Hills. This road is off I-85. I know Atlanta pretty well. On a regular traffic day, that's a thirty- to forty-minute drive. The U.S. citizen husband claims he'll be back to meet with us in fifteen minutes.

I explained to him there was no way that he could drive to North Druid Hills and back in fifteen minutes. That's at least an hour to an hour and a half roundtrip. I told him I did not want him to drive fast. I told him I was concerned about the validity of going to a doctor's office at 7:30 in the morning. I explained I did not know any doctors' offices that were open at 7:30 in the morning.

But he tells us he'll be there in fifteen minutes. OK, sure, we'll wait for you fifteen minutes. So we wait. My thinking was that he was not really going to the doctor's and was trying to buy time to get to me. We ended up waiting about thirty minutes. I called him back and asked what's his location was, if he thinks he's getting any closer, or if we can meet him somewhere closer.

He now tells me that he was getting close and he was only about 10 minutes away.

He tells me that he was speeding and was stopped by the police. Now he's getting a ticket for speeding. I tell him, "Maybe it's a better idea if you come into the office to talk."

The U.S. citizen agrees, and I thank him. We hung up, and my partner and I decided to drive back to the office.

As we're driving back to the office, we end up getting on Highway 78. He called me back, and I could hear that he was driving now. He didn't sound like he was driving before. The U.S. citizen's husband said, "I'm driving on Highway 78 right now."

I tell him, "That's amazing; we're driving on 78 as well." We're probably going to cross each other in a few minutes." He doesn't know where he's located on Highway 78. I asked him to meet me at the office. The U.S. citizen husband agrees to meet me at 9 a.m.

I am skeptical that he will show up after the runaround he gave me already.

At the time of the U.S. citizen husband case, I was part of the Document Benefit Fraud Task Force (DBFTF). I was assigned to an office with Homeland Security Investigations (HSI) across town. I spent most of my time there. Homeland Security Investigations has a lot more leeway to do investigations and dig deeper than we have at FDNS (Fraud Detection and National Security). HSI is able to look at social media. When I was working, we weren't allowed to look at anyone's social media. USCIS certainly wasn't allowed to use it against them, which I understand.

While I couldn't look up social media information on individuals, Homeland Security could, and I took advantage of that. I would simply ask investigators to look into these people for me. I would give HSI the names, give them what I knew about them, and they would do research for me on a lot of these individuals.

I never understood why we weren't allowed to do this in-depth research. We always thought that they didn't want us to catch anyone. It certainly seemed that way. Our management and our lawyers put up as many stumbling blocks in our way as possible. Most of the higher-ups were either ignorant of immigration, right-wing global corporatists, or leftists as you could get. That brew of mentality shaped the regulation and procedures for U.S. Immigration.

Our Office Chief Council (OCC) headquarters put every stumbling block they could in front of us. At some point, they did make social media available, but only at headquarters. So, you had to go through this funnel filter process to get any information, and they would block you ninety percent of the time. They did not want to help you, and they had few people on staff. You could imagine the results of 3,000 or 4,000 people requesting information from 10 people working at headquarters. Well, they weren't going to get you the information that you needed. To get it promptly in an active investigation wasn't possible. I was lucky enough to get my info from HSI.

This U.S. citizen husband had a broad social media signature. One of the things I noticed throughout his social media was images of shirtless men. The U.S. citizen husband also professed that he was a proud gay black man on his pages. There were no women whatsoever on any of his pages. He had a lot of pictures of himself. They were professionally made photos. He added tags in there that said so.

I didn't like being confrontational with people. There are other ways to get them to talk. My method was that I would flip through pages of documents and let them see the information while I was asking them certain questions that pertained to the information.

Ask them a question, let them answer, and then flip to a page that contradicts their answer. I had a bunch of the U.S. citizen husband's stuff printed out, and I asked him questions about his relationship and his life. I would flip the pages. Some pages were about his bills or taxes, things like that.

But then I started flipping pages of his online life. The fact that he was saying that he was gay. And this gentleman perked up, and he said, "Hey, those are my modeling photos."

I said, "Oh really? These are your photos?"

He says, "Yes."

I flipped the pages that showed photos with the caption on it where he says he's gay. He tells me, "Yes, I'm gay."

I went, "Really? Well, what does your wife think about you being gay?"

And he, of course, says, "She knows I'm gay. She's happy, she's fine with it." The U.S. citizen husband and model was sticking to his story of a viable marriage. He was not going to give it up.

Here's a technique that worked for me quite well being from the South. As a Southerner, I know something about our culture, it doesn't matter whether you're black, white, or Hispanic; if you're from the South ... we all share something in common. That's a reverence for our moms and our dads quite often. Sons for their moms and daughters for their dads. I was not above using that knowledge.

In the process of trying to get information from the U.S. citizen husband, I decided to use my parental technique. He would not give up the sham. I explained the penalties for committing fraud and the penalties for being involved in a fraudulent marriage. I let him read the penalties on the I-130 form that he signed. But then I simply asked him what his mother thought about his marriage. I said, "Does your mom know you're married?"

He said, "Yes, my mother knows that I am married, and she is fine with it." I said, "Great, well, listen. Why don't we give her a call and talk to her about your marriage and the fact that you're not living with your wife? She can tell me what she knows about your immigrant wife."

When I picked up the phone and started dialing her number, his face kind of dropped, he looked to be in shock that I might do that. He said, "Please don't call my mother. Please don't call my mother!"

"Well, listen, you permitted me to call your mother by signing off on the I-130 form. You gave me permission to contact anyone and ask anyone about your relationship, so I think I'm going to call your mother."

This thirty-year-old man dropped every pretense immediately. He started crying like a baby in front of me, begging and pleading with me not to call his mother. "Please don't call my mother. I've never been to jail. She will be so upset. I'm getting into so much trouble if you call my mother. I've never been in jail. I don't want to go to jail. Please don't call my mother."

I told him simply that it was time for him to come clean and tell me the truth so that I didn't have to call his mother.

He ended up telling me everything if I wouldn't call his mother. That was an easy denial for USCIS.

Walmart and Payless

I would be remiss if I didn't talk about Walmart. Walmart comes into the immigration picture for another reason. As with Kroger, Walmart has never done anything wrong, to my knowledge. I've never seen anything. I've never had reason to suspect or accuse Walmart of any illegal activity or illegal immigration at any time.

However, some of the people that work for Walmart at the store level have had some issues. Walmart wouldn't know this necessarily because they're employees. A few Walmart employees did assist marriage fraud arrangers, along with committing financial fraud, either to help the immigrants with credit card fraud, buy and sell different kinds of game cards, and/or funnel money through Walmart.

I had confessions from people who worked at Walmart. Immigrants would explain how some of their financial fraud worked and their relationships with employees inside Walmart. Financial fraud entry points were in the returns area of Walmart or in some of the cashiers that would help the scammers with credit card fraud, buy gift cards, large numbers of credit cards, and transferring money through either gift cards or credit cards.

Payless Shoes were used like Kroger. I had people that, for some reason, would also go to Payless Shoes and other shoe stores as well. They loved to take pictures of themselves buying shoes. So, you always had a married couple buying shoes, and you always wondered who was taking the pictures of them buying shoes. Sometimes, they would say it was someone in the store. Sometimes, their *cousin went with them. Always, the immigrants' cousin had gone with them to the shoe store. I suspected it was the marriage fraud arranger.*

The shopping malls were a big thing, too. What I often saw with the malls, well, they didn't actually go to the mall. The fraudulent marriage arranger, for some reason, instead of going to the mall, they would Photoshop themselves together in the mall, meaning that one of the group would actually go to the mall and they would somehow superimpose the husband and wife into the mall photo to make it look like they were at Payless Shoes. Most of the time, it was a terrible job and easy to tell. They weren't even professional at doing this. It was something to do. Payless was a place where scammers would love to Photoshop themselves and do a bad job of it, to boot.

I talk about Kroger, Walmart, and Payless because these are big stores that people know about, especially in the Southeast. But again, I want to emphasize that none of these stores had ever done anything wrong or criminal, and they're not the only places where this was done. They are the most memorable. I'd see fake employment letters from major gas stations as well, saying immigrants worked at the gas stations.

We saw a lot of that with Exxon, BP, and places like that where the applicant immigrants would send pay stubs to U.S. Immigration claiming to work for those companies. They didn't work for them at all. I think they used major companies because they assumed it would be hard to trace. People go to extremes to fake documents and try to portray their marriage as real.

Clothes Fairy

I always think that stories like these are kind of funny. In this case, the Atlanta office sent me a file of an applicant. They suspected a couple of being fraudulent, which is the reason I got it, my specialty. An older African American man (U.S. citizen) was married to an African female, with a large age gap between them. We've seen this before in previous stories. I prepped before the interview, trying to find out as much information about the two of them as I could. Do research on where they claim to live or, in some cases, where they might live. Also, do research to make sure you know where they work and if either the immigrant applicant or U.S. citizen is living with anyone else.

In this case, we determined that this gentleman lived in a senior living environment. He was retired or of retirement age.

I think I was at his house at about 6:00 a.m. I don't knock on people's doors at 6:00 a.m. unless I see lights on and movement and things like that. For this gentleman, we weren't too concerned because he was already retired.

My partner and I sat at this house until about 6:30 a.m. to see who would come or if there were lights on in the house. Now, the challenge on this stakeout was he lived at an apartment complex, determining if someone was active or not was more difficult. We decided to knock on the door. He came to the door, and we showed ID. We told him what we were there for and what we wanted to speak about.

We always request you to come in. So, he lets us in the door after we show him our credentials. I asked him where his claimed spouse was. He said, "She left for work." Of course, I asked him, "What time did she leave for work?"

He claimed she left about five minutes ago. He stated she was probably in the parking lot when we arrived. I explained that I was sitting outside about that time, I might have been there a little bit earlier than six, but I was right around that time, and I said I didn't see anyone leave.

Applicants always respond, "She must have left earlier than that, before you arrived, you probably just missed her."

We talked to him for a few minutes about his marriage. He called the spouse on the phone. She answered the phone and said she was on her way to work. You could tell from the phone conversation that it was on speaker and she was driving, there was a lot of wind and vehicle noise, things like that. She was probably going to work. She said on the phone that she was on the way to work and left the apartment.

We chatted with the male U.S. citizen for a few more minutes. Then I do my typical query, "Can you show me around the house?"

He agreed to show us around the house, and I asked him questions about where the claimed spouse keeps her clothes and such. I'll note that this was a small apartment. It was a one-bedroom apartment. There was a kitchen, a living room, and a bedroom. Of course, there was a bathroom and a small laundry area.

Before we got up to start looking around, I asked him one last question, "Where does she keep her clothes?" He said she keeps her clothes in the bedroom. That's good for me.

I asked, "Can you show me?" "Sure," he says.

We walked into the bedroom, and I asked him: "Which drawer is hers? Where does he keep his clothes? Where does she keep her other belongings?"

When we get to the bedroom, he states that her clothes are in the closet. I asked him to open the closet door. Mind you, this is not a big closet. It is a small closet with a door in it. He opens the closet, and there isn't any female clothes. Not a shred of female clothes, shoes, or anything feminine.

I do not know how he told me with a straight face that she had clothes in the closet. But he did, and then he actually showed me the closet. I turned to him after he did that, and I said, "Sir, you knew there were no women's clothes in the closet."

He smiled and shook his head. Then I asked, "Did you think the Clothes Fairy was going to come and miraculously put female clothes in your closet right before you opened the door?

He busted out laughing. It was so funny. I never used the Clothes Fairy line before.

I tell this story because I think it's funny, but unfortunately, this is a common thing. Almost **every** time I went out to the house to do a check, commonly called a "bed check," to make sure people live together, this is what you would find, or more accurately, not find. The U.S. citizen's room, most of the time, only had men's clothes because the younger immigrant woman's clothes were in the house with her actual husband, not the U.S. citizen who petitioned for them. The immigrants commonly lived with another man or woman, making for some comedic situations.

I'll share with you a couple of things that were common in the closets or drawers on the site visits to applicant's homes during the bed check:

There were neither male nor female clothes in any closet nor any drawer. The U.S. petitioner, female or male, had no clothes in the house.

Clothes Maketh
the Marriage

Often, we would run into various clothing issues. There might be a piece of clothing in the house that they could be able to present to you. I've had applicant immigrants hand me one shoe. "Could you show me the clothes that your husband has?" Nothing but one shoe, not even a pair of shoes. Sometimes one shoe, one bra, one shirt. The common answer to why one shoe or article of clothing was, "They must have taken all of their clothes with them; he or she left on Thursday." Or they would change their story to the husband or the wife left two days ago: "The truth is, we got in a fight, and he or she left two days ago."

And you go, "Really, a fight? And they took absolutely everything in the house that was theirs?"

Sometimes, the Opposite, Immigrants would have male and female clothes in the closet depending on who was there and who's not there, right? One of the things that a lot of the immigrant was trying to be smart or slick, they'd go to Goodwill or a thrift store and buy a bunch of stuff. If they're supposed to be married to a U.S. citizen man, they'd buy a bunch of male clothes. If they're supposed to be married to a woman, they'd buy women's clothes regardless of the size. Some drawers or closets may have ten different sizes in them. And how do you know that they went to Goodwill? They would have a stack of clothes, five shirts, and six pairs of pants or something like that, and they didn't even bother to take the tags off, still with the gleaming Goodwill tag.

After some research and finding the immigrant petitioner most likely lived at another address, it wasn't uncommon for me to go inside the immigrant's actual house and see her real husband's clothing and apparel. Here's a short story illustrating that scenario.

In one case, the male U.S. citizen was 5'4" tall. He probably weighed 120 or 130 pounds soaking wet. Now the immigrant's female's real husband was probably 6'2" and roughly 240 pounds, a pretty decent size guy, right? I asked to see the clothes in the closet. All the clothes were XXL (extra-extra-large), and the shoes were like size eleven.

I asked her, "Your U.S. husband told me he has been wearing size nine shoes. The closet has size eleven shoes, which are too big for me. I wear a size ten in my shoe." But she didn't get that. These are some of the things you run into.

The other good one, if there weren't any clothes, as you'd get answers like: "They must have taken all their clothes to the laundry," even though they have a washer and dryer in the house; "My spouse must have moved the clothes, they might be in the laundry room," and of course, you got to the laundry room, and there were no clothes.

The Clothes Fairy giveth and taketh.

Colonel for Asylum

This is an asylum case. This was not originally my case. I was contacted by *Customs and Border Patrol* (CPB) regarding a gentleman who lived in Atlanta. This gentleman was from Nigeria. He was a naturalized U.S. citizen. And he had been to his home country of Nigeria and was now coming back to the U.S. On the return flight, he landed in Houston, Texas. This gentleman was flagged because Homeland Security was looking at old cases where people may have obtained citizenship through fraudulent means. This gentleman's fingerprints came back as being associated with two different names tied to immigration applications.

These two applications linked to this man were both asylum applications. I picked this case up after his filing based on interviews conducted by CBP at the Houston Port of Entry. I was asked to go out and talk to him about his multiple applications. An HSI agent was unable to contact the man in the field. We were fortunate the gentleman came into the office to be interviewed. I'd completed some site visits trying to find out where he lived. I went to his house; a lady was there. She would not open the door; she talked to us through a window. This sometimes happens, and that was OK as long as she was talking. Well, fortunately, this gentleman voluntarily came into my office.

We sat down in a room with s three chairs and a circular desk. It's kind of like an interrogation; however, we don't call it interrogation at DHS; we call it an interview. I won't bore you with the details, but one of the things we always have to do is, we have to tell them who we are. We show credentials and explain the reason for the interview. We also have to explain to them that interviews are strictly voluntary and they're free to go, they can leave at any time. They can cut it off and leave; they don't have to stay with us. This interview process lasted about an hour. I recorded the interview. I repeated four times that he was free to go and that the interview was voluntary. Throughout the interview, I told him that he was free to go. I reminded him that the doors were not locked, and one of the doors went directly into the lobby. He could walk out the door from there. Throughout the interview, he contradicted himself and told odd stories, changing his story and blaming his brother for the mix-up.

I'd researched the man and had his two files together. This gentleman had come into the United States using a certain name in New York City while filing for asylum.

His story went something like this: He was a middle-ranking Air Force officer in Nigeria. He further stated that the government was corrupt and the president at the time was corrupt. So he and some of his fellow officers decided to get together and topple the Nigerian government and started protesting. They were looking to do a coup d'état, trying to overthrow the government. He was caught and fortunate enough to sneak away and come to the United States. Of course, this was not good grounds for asylum.

He was afraid for his life. He thought the government was going to kill him because he had taken part in this potential coup. It ended up being a lengthy story. The asylum officers in New York did not believe his story and the asylum officer sent his file to an asylum judge (an immigration judge). That's the way it works. If the asylum officer doesn't believe you, they don't deny you; they put you in a proceeding so you can go see a judge. This way, you get a second chance for asylum before you're denied. The judge makes that final decision. Of course, if the judge doesn't agree and denies the asylum claim, then you are ordered to be removed. That still is not the end. You can appeal to the Board of Immigration Appeals, essentially a third chance. This process is long, and it takes years to be removed; it's costly, and **everyone** appeals because it is so lengthy. We have been talking for eight to ten years. Anyway, they did that; they sent him a notice to appear (NTA) before an immigration judge. We colloquially changed the name of the NTA to a *notice to run* because when people get these, they run. They leave immediately and flee somewhere else because they figured the judge or someone can't find them in a new district or area. Because they run, their hearing process goes in front of a judge, and they're automatically ordered to be deported. In this Nigerian Air Force case, the judge ordered him deported. But since he ran and he ran quickly, no one could find him.

The Nigerian Air Force guy had gone to Tampa, Florida. When he was in Tampa in the South Florida area, he amazingly filed for asylum again. This time, he used a different name and a new cover story as a Christian minister. His story was that he worked as a pastor of a church in a predominantly Muslim half of Nigeria. There are a lot of conflicts between the two. Mostly, they seem to get along well, but there are issues. Think about Boka Haram. Well, this gentleman says that he lived in a predominantly Muslim area, and he was a Christian minister. He was spreading the gospel, and the Muslims didn't like that; according to him, the Muslims were going to kill him, and they threatened him. Thus giving him a reason for asylum in the USA. This scenario was much sounder as asylum grounds. He was now a protected class, being persecuted for religious reasons. The Nigerian government did nothing about it. He was playing on this fear of Islam and Muslim people. Well, this time, the asylum officer in Florida believed him. Now, this was a time when we didn't have the best systems to identify fraudsters in place. This was an old case; thus, we didn't have the checks that we do today. Fraudsters know to apply again quickly because those links don't come up. This time, Tampa Asylum granted him the benefit. Now, he was set and was on his way to becoming a U.S. citizen.

His Nigerian wife had done the same thing, but she was not granted asylum at any time. She had used a different name in her filing. But she was denied and ended up leaving the country before the immigration judge removed her, or so he said. I think she was living under the radar with him for years. His grown children were here. The woman in the window was about his wife's age. I could not prove it, but it was possible.

At that point in the story, he's a U.S. citizen who has now been granted citizenship, coming into the office; however, fingerprints matched both names he used. We merged the files with the matching fingerprints, and this is where we were. So this gentleman gets placed in criminal proceedings, he lied under oath to a federal agency, and he still is going to obtain U.S. citizenship through fraudulent means. It's a serious offense.

Because of that, he went to trial. He wanted a jury trial; before this, we gave him a chance to plead out, and he didn't. So, he went to trial. His defense attorney decided that they were going to fight the interview that I had done with him. They claimed that I threatened him and that I was trying to intimidate him. The thing is, he never admitted to anything to me, so I didn't understand what they were arguing. You could pretty much surmise that he lied during my interview because his story changed so much that I picked away at his answers.

He stood by his story all the way. What he did tell me was that the person who had filed in New York wasn't him; it was his brother. It wasn't him; he didn't do it. Ironically, it was a mistaken identity defense from a fraudulent applicant. When I explained to him that his fingerprints were the same as his brother's fingerprints, he stuck by that story. He wasn't willing to admit that he had committed fraud and never did so. I wasn't sure what they were about to argue with my testimony in court. I had audio-taped his interview, and I had typed everything verbatim. The judge could see that I offered this gentleman four or more times the voluntary right to exit. He was free to go at any time. I instructed him where the door was and that the door was not locked, so the judge kind of threw that argument out. The judge confirmed it was strictly voluntary, and the gentleman was allowed to leave; he was provided with an explanation of his right to walk out free and not under arrest. So, we went on to trial, and he chose to testify in the trial hearing. The CBP (Customs and Border Patrol) testified. A man from the forensic document lab testified on signatures, and a forensic document lab fingerprint specialist came down and testified that both sets of fingerprints belonged to him.

Now, the interesting thing I got from the U.S. attorney was that the jury didn't believe my testimony; additionally, the jury did not believe the forensic document fingerprint specialist's testimony. The jury did not believe the federal officer's testimony; they were skeptical that everyone had an individual set of fingerprints (a well-known fact). This made conviction kind of a challenge. The U.S. attorney was a little bit frightened that this guy was going to walk. This was when police were under heightened scrutiny from everyday media coverage of law enforcement being abusive and lying, making all law enforcement prosecutions difficult and a challenge.

This gentleman decided that he was going to take the stand, I would assume against his own attorney's recommendation, but he got on the stand and testified. The prosecutor did a cross-examination of him. They questioned him. He told his story on the stand. He got on the stand, and the jury didn't believe him. His stories were so far-fetched and unreasonable that they got him convicted during a time of scrutiny for law enforcement and prosecution.

After the trial and the jury found him guilty, he went back to his jail cell pending a final conviction and sentencing. While he was awaiting his sentence, he was throwing a fit in prison, as the guards told us. He was making phone calls and explaining what he was trying to do to look like he was crazy. He was a diabetic and refused to take his medicine to physically show he wasn't just acting. As legend has it, he would stand in the middle of his cell completely nude and rub his feces all over himself to try to get out of prison.

Telephone calls in prison are monitored and recorded. He should have known this. The prison staff told them that their telephone calls were recorded. In his telephone calls, he was saying that he was doing this intentionally. He wasn't crazy, reiterating he was doing this because he was faking being crazy. He wanted to show enough craziness so he could get out of prison and run once again.

But somehow, during the process and two weeks before his being sentenced and convicted, he faced the final judgment by dying in prison. I do not know the full circumstances. I suspect it was because he did not take his diabetes seriously.

Because he died in prison, he was never convicted and was never sentenced. It was as if the trial never occurred. He didn't lose his citizenship, which he was relentlessly trying not to do. Being a citizen, not convicted, makes all his spouse eligible for certain benefits. One of those was his wife, who was also defrauding the United States. I don't know if she left; what I do know is he lived with a woman who claimed to be his wife. Confusing, yes, but that's the game to beat the system. It's confusing, but that might have been his wife in this country. He could have had more than one wife in this country; he was petitioning for another wife. We thought this was the wife who had been ordered deported from the United States. Maybe she never left, as far as we know, but the interesting thing is that a petition was pending for her. And he died without being convicted or his citizenship removed. She potentially was eligible for adjustment as the widow of a U.S. citizen and could have gotten benefits through that. That could quickly happen and slip through the cracks, as most of them do. But I thought that it was interesting that she was now eligible, possibly a final win for the guy who died in prison relentlessly trying to keep his U.S. citizenship.

Employment and Business Fraud

I've written about a lot of marriage fraud and a little bit about employment fraud. This is a story about employment fraud that I ran into early in my career. I'll try to give you a brief background of how some people come into this country without getting into the technicalities and legalities of it. Companies can petition for individuals to come into the United States. Generally, they try to petition people with specific skills. One of the primary ways that people are petitioning for employment-based entry is for the IT industry, computer engineers, and things of that nature, and the other is for farm workers and agricultural businesses.

There is a lot of misinformation about how these petitions work. For instance, in the agricultural business, people often talk as if these are for people to live here permanently. Farm workers come here for a specific amount of time and then go back to their country. Generally, those farm workers only come here for about six months. They come in April; they leave in September. Somewhere in that warm season, they come in to help plant the crops, then they work the fields, and then they help harvest the crops, and they go home. In South Georgia, for instance, a lot of those people were patient farm workers. We always think of Central America and Mexico, but the truth is a lot of them fly in and fly out.

Another group that comes into the country is the American managers. Companies can petition for people: nurses, managers, and business managers in certain fields and in certain areas to run companies. When I first started, this was used a lot by Indians, Middle Easterners, and Koreans as a method to enter the country permanently.

Koreans owned a lot of dry-cleaning businesses. And quite a few of the Indians either owned gas stations or sandwich shops, Blimpie's, and Subway sandwich shops. In both instances, what they would do is, let's say, I own dry cleaner A. Someone else owns dry cleaner B. Dry-cleaning company A would petition for the owner of dry-cleaning company B as my manager. Company A petitions for the owner of Company B to be the manager.

Now, the craziest part about these petitions is that none of these people ever actually worked for the other person. They're only being petitioned by that company. The person gets granted a visa to work here. And in this instance, they can get granted an adjustment of status to become a permanent resident to live and work for that company. Once the companies file a petition and they have been approved, the person from company B files to become a resident. Company A writes a letter and says they still want to hire them. Then, the Company B manager can become a permanent resident.

This system worked the same way for the gas stations and the sandwich shops. Keep in mind that none of these people ever actually went to work for the other company. I'm sure you're going to ask me how I know. Well, at some point, all those people would come in to get their citizenship. And when you look through the records, and they brought in their new information, they never worked for the petitioning company, not one day. When you ask them why they didn't work for them, every one of them said the same thing: "The other company took too long to get my green card, and so the other company hired someone else."

Now, that sounds plausible, right? But it's untrue. The reason it's untrue is the moment that those individuals applied to become permanent residents; they're allowed to get an employment authorization card to work. They get that before they get an adjustment of status. So, every one of them could have gone to work for that petitioning company immediately. But none of them did. The way the law works, it's such a loophole that there's nothing you can do about it. It was for years, one of the biggest scams going on in Atlanta. Yet it was perfectly legal.

Eight-year-old Vice President

For me, one of the strangest filings that I had was not an Indian or Korean. This filing pertained to a young Mexican man. This young man was twenty-one years old and was born in 1982. A Mexican restaurant in the Atlanta area filed for him. The restaurant had hired him to be the manager. I believe his uncle owned the restaurant.

I can give you a little more background about the employment-based process. If someone wanted to hire someone who was a foreigner, they had to apply with the Department of Labor. At the time, the form was called an ETA 750. The only thing that's changed in this process is they changed the name of the form. It's now an ETA 9089. The company would file this form with the Department of Labor, and it said the company wants to hire this person for this amount of money to do this job in this field. The fields usually pertain to fields that the Department of Labor had said there weren't enough workers. The company had to prove that they couldn't find a worker here, which was not that hard to do. They also had to show they could pay the wages necessary for the job.

This company had filed an ETA 750, and the Department of Labor had approved it for this young man. I'm looking through his application, and I'm reading through his ETA750, his petition, and his high 485 adjustments of application. This gentleman, by the way, had an attorney with him who had filed and completed all the paperwork.

In his application, it showed that he had started working for a food distribution company in Mexico in 1984. In 1986, he was promoted to supervisor. He was an amazing worker. In 1988 he was made the manager of the shipping department within the distribution center. By 1990, he was promoted to vice president of this distribution company. He oversaw international sales and shipping within the company of its products.

The Department of Labor granted The ETA 750 partly based on this information.

The ETA 750 was approved. They filed a visa petition for him to come here and work. The Petition was filed at the Texas Service Center, where labor petitions were processed. The Texas Service Center reviewed this petition, showing the gentleman's age when he was born in 1982. The Texas Service Center granted this petition for this gentleman.

After the grant of the petition, the gentleman and his attorney filed the I-485 adjustment status, and that's where I came in. I'm interviewing this young man with his attorney present. I review all this information. It is sometimes difficult to stay completely professional. How do you maintain a straight face when talking to someone and hearing this story?

So, I asked the gentleman how he managed to start working at this distribution center when he was two years old and become a supervisor by the time he was four, and become vice president by the time he was eight years old.

His attorney interjected by this time. And she said, "Officer Lee, I'm sorry. That's a mistake. My mistake. I put down the wrong dates."

I, of course, want to know what the new dates were that she came up with.

I give her a piece of paper and let her confer with her client. She writes down new dates for me. In the new dates, this gentleman was now working in the Distribution center in 1990. He was made a supervisor in 1992, a manager in 1994, and the vice president of the company in 1996. This, of course, prompts me to ask more questions. I asked him what grade he finished in school. He told me that he had gone to school until he was twelve years old.

I commented to the attorney that I was amazed. At the time, I had a fourteen-year-old son of my own who was smart. Today, he's an engineer. But at the time, I said, "I'm surprised that this gentleman has become the Vice president of a company without finishing past the equivalent of the seventh grade. And my son hasn't mastered getting himself up for school yet."

I explained to both that I wasn't sure about this application and that I could not approve it at the time. I was straightforward to them that I was going to send this back to the service center and see if they would revoke it because it was not a properly filed application. It made no sense whatsoever.

The Department of Labor DOL dealt with ETA 750s and the labor certification in their Atlanta office. I called DOL to discuss this application with them. I explained the application and explained to the DOL supervisor my age issues. I asked if they looked at these applications at all.

I was talking to the lady that managed the ETA 750 program. She told me that they didn't look at fraud. They weren't concerned about fraud. She said, "We thought immigration investigated the fraud."

I explained to her The DOL had jurisdiction over the ETA 750. The Department of Labor was responsible for reviewing those applications. That at the time, which was legacy, the Immigration Naturalization Service had no jurisdiction over the ETA 750. I further explained that because she was a federal agency, granting these people approvals was difficult for us to go back on them and find anything else because we are not the Department of Labor. Basically, in her conversation, that's when I realized that the Department of Labor was not the Department of Labor; it was the Department of Corporations.

This was not the only odd ETA 750 I ever saw. There were a lot of these different variations and different issues that went on with them. The Department of Labor rubber-stamped everything that came across their desk. I firmly believe everyone in that department had no clue what they were doing and had no interest in learning. I worked with a DOL investigator, and he complained about his own people constantly. After years of this, I realized the DOL cared nothing for American workers and only for American Corporations.

Field of Dreams

In the employment-based process, companies can file for individuals to come here and work. A lot of these companies are small companies. Small IT companies are primarily what I've dealt with, but first, I'll tell you about large companies I've dealt with.

I mainly deal with Indian companies. Indian individuals would enter the U.S. and create startup companies. Supposedly, what they're going to do is hire people to develop software programs. They're going to create, sell, and advance U.S. industry.

In my experience, the truth is that 90% of immigrant programmers and companies had fake software development. I'd hear, "Oh, I need to bring people in to help me create this program." I can tell you I never saw one completed program or significantly developed software in hundreds of site visits to these immigrant software companies. Many companies ran this scam for years and years.

These fake companies would usually bring in up to twenty or thirty people. That may not seem like a lot, but you have hundreds of outfits doing it in Atlanta and thousands doing it across the United States. It adds up over time.

The way that the scam works, the first thing they've got to do is show that no U.S. citizen is willing to take that job. Some of the common schemes to show no U.S. citizen is willing to fill the jobs are taking out classified ads in obscure papers with few readers, or they will advertise on internet sites and tell specific individuals when it will be posted and how to get there so they are first in line to be hired.

Most commonly, they will advertise the job at $65,000 per year. For an IT computer engineer with five years of experience, the going rate is mid to high six figures. So, no American will apply. Indeed.com lists the industry standard salaries of those positions. Most large companies pay their workers on the high end, somewhere between $160,000 -$193,000 per year. It is much cheaper to contract these jobs out, even using 1099 to hire foreign workers, because then companies do not have to pay Social Security taxes, Medicare, and federal and state taxes. This can save them anywhere from 20 to 30 percent.

So, let's separate the three fraud techniques. The first one (advertised in an obscure newspaper) was fairly cut and dry. How does that benefit the scammer? When you do a location/site visit, one of the things you asked for is proof that they've advertised at all and asked for supporting documents and receipts. Then, we ask investigative questions to the company hiring the foreign applicants: How did you know these immigrants applying? How did you apply for these people to come? What steps did you take in the application process? So you look at their records and documents added to their file. In the old days, the company would hand us the actual classifieds (jobs section) and newspaper clippings for the position. Typically, the companies would find the smallest and most obscure newspaper to advertise the job in and tip off the immigrant to go look at the job section listed in the paper. By the way, the heads of the companies were also advertising in India to keep a steady flow of immigrant software workers into the country. The advertisement in India was more prominent than in the USA to tip the scales for more migrant software developers.

The second (posting on Internet sites) you'd think would be self-explanatory; however, tracking the authenticity of this sometimes shady but effective H-1B system became more difficult on the Internet because a company advertising in foreign countries cannot be easily tracked.

You find out this information from immigrants themselves, of individuals working for the Petitioning Company. The petitioning companies are essentially software human traffickers for H-1B mill operators. The petitioners ask the potential H-1B visa applicant to respond to ads on foreign sites, then prep them for identical job ads in the U.S.

The third one (lowballing the salary) is the big one. The more experience you have, the more knowledge you have of different software systems and different programming languages, and the more it increases your wealth and worth. Shockingly, the word on the software street from shady H-1B mill operators was the flooding of U.S. markets with global workers from underdeveloped countries would drive six-figure U.S. software jobs, one of the mainstays of modern America to the salary level of landscapers.

I worked on a lot of these cases from 2017 to 2019. The companies formed to bring in H-1B applicants would advertise a job for $65,000, which was the standard low-end rate in Atlanta. Not the standard going rate but the low end of the U.S. Department of Labor's guide for what their salary should be. In no way was it market competitive at the time. The companies would advertise for $65K with a requirement of five years of experience. Essentially, anyone with five years of experience or more in the United States wouldn't even apply for that job. H-1B immigrants who were here already and established weren't going to quit their jobs to switch for a lower salary, either.

Why wouldn't the new arrivals bolt on the $65,000 job per year after arrival? First of all, the new H-1B arrivals may have a questionable track record. Secondly, the companies would offer the new arrivals $65,000 a year, then promise a bonus at the end of the year. They'd pay the new immigrants $65,000 a year salary, and then in December of **every** year, they gave them a bonus. If they met their quota, the bonuses would be anywhere from $35,000 to $65,000 to put their salary in line with the going rate. But it was done on purpose to exclude Americans from the job, and that was the driving force.

I know it's hard to comprehend some of this. Over my career, I've done hundreds of site visits to these types of companies. It's hard for me to understand fully. I have been to small companies to companies with 300+ employees, and the only American person in the entire corporation was the face of the company, the press secretary, or the person who speaks to the public. Any other company that only hires one ethnic group would be considered a racist company under the values and norms of our society. But not in this situation. Even claiming it as I do makes me reluctant.

The backlash will be severe. But the truth is the truth. Regardless of a homogenous worksite going against the current norms of our society, this plot and systemic action of undermining the American worker happened to all U.S. citizens, no matter what religion, national origin, race, color, or creed.

I mention $65,000. Well, that is what the Department of Labor (what I like to refer to as the Department of Corporations) considers the prevailing wage in the IT industry. Never mind that it is a bullshit number that some bureaucrat pulled out of their ass. This number has no real correlation to what is going on in the real-world marketplace.

Indian Employment Scams

My first big one was a bank in Atlanta, it was one of the largest in the U.S. It was a big enterprise in Atlanta, covering several office floors in one facility, a large bank's IT operation. On the third story of the building, we went into an enormous room with 250 desks. Every desk wasn't filled, but there were a lot of people working, about a hundred.

Of the 100 working at the time, approximately ninety-nine of them emigrated from India, and one African American man who I spoke to sat in the far corner away from the others. There were no other Americans; everyone else had been immigrants petitioned to become legal permanent residents or were in the process of being petitioned. There were no Americans outside of the one gentleman; everybody up the food chain was seen as foreign-born. It was the same for the smaller H-1B visa software trafficking mill companies flooding U.S. markets with unneeded labor. Once again, the face of the company, the PR guy, and the HR guy were Americans. The bank outsourced its IT department from an American tech company that ran this type of setup throughout the country, including only hiring people from India. Everybody knew about it, but nobody cared.

So I probed and prodded a little bit to ask some questions about this clear absence of American workers. One of the questions I began to ask anytime I would go out was, "There are five well-known tech universities in Atlanta: Georgia State, Mercer, Emory, Georgia Tech, and DeVry University, among many others. Why aren't you hiring anyone from those top schools?"

All of these universities have major IT programs, and you, Mr. IT Company, couldn't find one American citizen to work for you?

Not one of them ever said, "No, we can't. Any H-1B company designed to bring in foreign workers to undercut American wages wouldn't give a clear answer in all the years that I asked that question. Every corporate exec would smile at me and shrug their shoulders. But I never got a definitive "no," which is to me, a sign of deception. They wouldn't answer the question. Now, if they prepped and were ready for you to come in, and especially if they sensed the media might expose them, they'd give you a good answer, but you could still catch them on the spot.

In another case, I talked to one gentleman immigrant working for this vast entity. I asked him what his job was going to be. What was he doing for the H-1B visa?

He replied, "I'm a computer programming engineering technical guy." He didn't have any super skills but was working on a specific program for the financial markets. Regardless, he wasn't a specialist.

To make matters worse, he was trained by the company that petitioned for him. He didn't get this skill inside a university or a software company in India. He was specifically trained to do the financial markets project and certainly did not have five years of experience. He had five years of experience in IT offices, but not in this field of programming. Any U.S. citizen could have been trained in basic programming to do the work.

These immigrants make a lot of money, and the individuals do get paid well. Then, why do these companies go through all of this trouble? Financial and tech companies lean toward the Left and are progressives, Democrats. They also tend to favor open borders.

As a Democrat growing up, we were the Pro-Labor, "protect the jobs" party. I'll tell you why certain banks and tech companies are trending toward hiring H-1B immigrants instead of U.S. citizens: because if the bank had to hire them as actual full-time employees, they would have to pay health insurance, worker's comp, liability insurance, Social Security, and more taxes. They would be responsible for the Americans as individual employees. Certain companies don't want to do that; they want to get away with cheap labor, paying as little as possible. So, they contract out to companies that specialize in H-1B visas at the expense of the American worker. It seems more expensive and chaotic, but the big caveat is the banks, telecoms, and tech companies that go down that road don't have to keep that person on for any length of time, which can be used to minimize labor costs and unfortunately, stop core career jobs for Americans.

While these individuals make good money, they don't get any healthcare insurance because they're contractors. Most in the Department of Labor don't really care about labor; they certainly don't care about employees (isn't that a political policy above the Department of Labor?). All of this facilitates a lack of connection between the H-1B contractors and the companies. If the visa immigrants make $65,000 a year, the going immigrant rate at the time, there's no concern or affinity to the company since they won't be there long anyway. It's a manifestation of the corporate policy eliminating long-term career positions from loyal working American citizens originally in those IT positions. Even when these individuals make only $65,000 a year, it is still a hell of a lot better than the wages in India.

These Indian brokerage companies and petitioning companies overwhelm the immigration process. They take advantage of both the immigrants and the American workers.

Not all of the Indian companies that funnel H-1B workers into the U.S. are large immigration mills. Most of my visits were to small mom-and-pop firms that also focused on H-1B visa immigrants, like the big companies. I'll try to break it down as simply as I can for you on how these work. There are massive numbers of these small mom-and-pop immigration micro mills bringing in IT workers from India.

Every time I went out, I'd see the same thing. First, you'd have an H-1B petitioner coming to work for a small company and asking for a U.S. immigration officer. Usually, the boss at the mom-pop company would have ten or twelve people working there. There was enormous turnover, so the boss was petitioning people all the time.

1) The immigration H-1B immigration boss works out of a small virtual office. A virtual office is hosted in a large building with tiny offices rented out to small companies. They're big enough for a person, one computer, and a printer table. All the businesses at the virtual office have access to a common area to hang out with others and a conference room where you can book a time if needed. Called virtual offices because generally, no one works out

of the office. For the most part, it gives you an address and a mail drop. That's its only purpose.

For immigration purposes, it gives the entity that is petitioning for individuals a place to say that they work out. The mom-and-pop company usually says, "I'm hiring this individual to work out of my virtual office to develop the software program for my company." That sounds OK, right, I mean, it is one guy. But that person who petitioned for a visa never works at an office. And the boss doesn't petition for one person over the years; he's probably petitioned for 100 people. All the petitions are for people to work on software that already exists or to work in a completely different IT field or other companies that are already in existence.

2) The mom-and-pop boss usually contracts with another party to hire the immigrant software engineer he helped to come into this country, and then that next person hires him out to someone else to work at another agency; it's this huge kind of pyramid scheme. And each person along the way gets money, and corporate America saves money by doing this, why? Again, the major corporations at the top of the pyramid scheme don't have to hire the person directly, they don't have to pay Social Security, and through a contractor worker, they're exempt from many laws, rules, taxes, or regulations. And I'm always fascinated when leftists and right-wing corporatists talk about people doing jobs that no one wants to take. The reality's a scam and a fraud, and they don't have to pay people normally. Mind you, this person has done this for years and years and years, claiming that he's hiring people to create some special program or software or something. And that software never gets developed, ever.

3) We talked about the common use of virtual offices. But we also have "pretend offices." A pretend office is someone who says that they have an office they're hiring people to come work in and develop software. They've got this whole new product that they want to create. It's always new software that they're creating. When you look at this company, or you look at what they're doing, you'll see that they work in two different places: one, they work out of their home, or they have no office space at all. It is all fiction.

I went to a site visit in Huntsville, Alabama, about two hours from the Atlanta office, looking for an office of 100 employees supposedly working there. So I left early in the morning, and I finally found the office building in Huntsville. Fortunately for me, it's right next to a gas station. I'd been driving for two hours; I needed something to drink. It gave me a minute to sit there and think to myself about the case. I looked through the file on this particular case. Again, typical software engineer. This company has filed for over 100 employees from India to work out of this office that developed this software and to become an upstanding part of society. One of the first things I noticed in the building where these individuals work is a chain on the front door. This building is old. There's a sign for the company on the front door. It looks like a little copy of a piece of paper with the name of the company on it. You can look right through the glass door, and there is nothing inside. It's an open cavernous room through the back of the brick building. You can look through the windows, but there's nothing there. The ceiling is falling, and some of the lights have fallen. It looks pretty rough like nobody's been in there in quite a while. I walk around to the side of the building; there are stairs going up to the top. I walk up the stairs to see if anyone is upstairs or if that door is possibly open, and maybe there's a big room upstairs with employees.

I banged on the door and knocked, doing everything I could to see if anyone would come and open the door. No one came to the door. It appeared that the electricity worked; however, nothing was going on in this building. So I called the owner of this company. The same owner of the company that's supposed to be petitioning for H-1B visa status for his people. I explained that I'm a U.S. immigration officer here to ask questions and if the immigrant he was petitioning for is available to speak.

The owner says, "Certainly."

The business owner explained to me that he was in Dallas at that time and he was unable to talk to his immigrant employee, "But you're welcome to call the office, and they'll be glad to talk."

I confirmed the address for the office. It's the address where I'm standing at an empty building. I asked the business owner to reconfirm that this particular person he's petitioned for is working in the office.

He said yes.

I then explained to the business owner that I was sitting outside of his "office."

He's a little bit stunned; he stuttered and stammered for a few minutes.

And I asked, "Why are you sure that he's inside the building?"

'The business owner's response is, "Yes, of course he's in there."

Is there any way that someone could come out to the door and open the door for me? Yes, they should; someone should come." So, we go on with this routine for a few minutes.

I finally tell him, "Sir, this building is abandoned. It's about to fall, and there's no one in this office space at all."

In two seconds, he goes, "Oh my God, they must have moved."

I swear, I said, "Are you kidding? You own this company, and you don't even know that your company has moved."

I asked him for the phone number of the H-1B immigrant who was supposed to be working for him to verify his moving claim. He asked that I give him a minute to call his secretary and get the information. I agreed to this and told him I would stand by for his call.

I called his H-1B immigrant employee before the business owner could call. He told me that he was working at that empty office in that space and told me what software he was building.

I asked him to come to the door.

Then he changed his story and said he was working from home that day.

The owner called me back in about five minutes and told me he was mistaken and that the person I was looking for had decided not to take the job. So, he was not working for the company.

I explained that I spoke to the employee, and he said he did work for the company. We must have had a bad connection because the phone line immediately cut off. Funny, but this happened to me often. Bad connections when you provide bad news.

Employment Millionaires

Just to give you some idea of how much money there is to be made in H-1B immigration fraud, let's say I have ten employees that I'm bringing into the country. The mom-and-pop immigration mill boss runs through employees quickly because once they get status, the immigrant moves on to more legitimate work. Plus, they don't pay them as well as they could. They don't get all the benefits that they could from larger agencies or if the immigrants were a full-time employee with a big company. So they have to keep a constant flow or conveyer belt of new people coming in. The mom-and-pop immigration mill owners don't care because they're going to use them for a year, maybe two years, and move on because the turnover causes a lack of need for sustainable benefits, so they're looking to move on to the next immigrant. Even more lucrative, an immigrant mill boss gets a contract to bring in a person that gets paid $65,000-$110,000. The boss contracts out this person for well over $130,000; the H-1B pyramid scheme pays in gold. That next person will contract out that same employee to another company for $160,000. That last contractor is going to be paying him the immigrant.

As I previously mentioned, the boss brings the immigrant in and pays that person $65,000. But he's probably going to pay him closer to $100,000 from the end-of-the-year bonus. If the mill boss contracts the H-1B immigrant out to a large company, outsourcing at the market rate of $150,000/year, then the Boss makes $50,000. Now you calculate that out twenty times a year, and the boss makes a cool $1 million. The immigrant mill boss keeps the factory conveyer belt going nonstop for a steady stream of people coming into the United States, subverting how the law is supposed to work and taking high-paying American career positions. And remember, all of these immigrant mill companies claim that they're building their software to hire immigrants in the first place, but they never are.

If You Can't Make It, Steal It

Some of the companies that do this are sufficiently large enough that they have office space. Fairly large office space. I would run into immigrants in actual office spaces that were set up as learning centers. These more sophisticated bosses bring in people from overseas who have a specific contract with a major bank or a supply chain distribution center. Major corporations that run complicated IT systems. The bosses train them in specific software for these companies. Now, they're supposed to be bringing immigrants in because they're already skilled and trained to fill a job where there are no Americans able to. As usual, that's not the case. Big immigrant bosses bring them in, train them, and send them to work at a major company through a third-party contractor and haul in the proceeds.

I was talking to a buddy of mine from the Department of State (DOS). We did quite a few cases together over the years. He reminded me of this one case we did together.

The big boss owner of this company had submitted a lot of information about the software program that he was developing. I was sent schematics and a lot of stuff about the software architecture of the program, which is kind of unusual. Through research, we found that the software the immigrant big boss had his team develop was actually software created, developed, and in use by a company out of New York. I mean the exact code from the New York Company's software. So I'd been tasked to go out and see this place. I went out to the owner's offices in Atlanta. He wasn't there; he was in Colorado. When I spoke to him on the phone, he was trying to drum up new work in Colorado. This was, of course, after I'd already done a site visit. At the H-1B immigrant Atlanta office, the owner had an office and the receptionist had an office (even though there wasn't a receptionist or a computer), and a couple of people were working in the main area. So someone came up to see me. And I spoke to an individual who had gotten his legal permanent residence through another company, doing the same software work with another group. He gave me a tour of the office space, which was a pretty good size. And the offices were not offices at all; they were classrooms. Each one of them was set up as a classroom, and each one of them was teaching a different aspect of this software that the New York Company already developed. There were four people in the entire building. I spoke to each one of them. After the first guy gave me the tour, the other three petitioned for H-1B visas from the big boss's company at this location. In the last room that I went into, there was a huge whiteboard that covered the whole right side of the wall with an enormous amount of computer programming language written on it. At the top left corner of the giant whiteboard was the actual name of the software that the company in New York had developed, and when I spoke to the immigrant petitioners, I asked them about it.

"Are you developing any software for this company?"

Every one of them said, "No, we don't develop software; we're just using this software."

"What software do you use? What do you do, and what is the purpose of this office space?"

And every one of them said that we use this software out of New York, and we're training to be able to write the program and basically to do corrections on it. So, what they were doing was working out the kinks and developing little things to help make the process run smoothly and working on eliminating glitches. That's all they did, and none of them had any clue of any software being developed, yet all of them had been petitioned to do exactly that.

All of them said that they would eventually be farmed out into different parts of the country to work on this software for different companies. Most of the people who worked out of that company were doing the same thing, but no one was working on any new software development, contradicting the whole purpose of all of their petitions.

I reached out to the owner again because he was still in Colorado, and I asked him if he would set up another appointment when he got back into town. We arranged the meeting for two weeks. So when I came back to the office, my buddy from the Department of State and a good buddy of mine from the Department of Homeland Security decided we'd all go out together.

It's a typical routine of asking questions. We went through our routine with the big boss, and he stood by his story, after repeated questioning, that he was creating the software program that was going to be developed and had been working on it for five years. I asked him to show me the software.

I asked the big boss to show me the software that he was developing. He agreed, and we walked down the hall into what he claimed was his server room. When we walked in, I saw that his servers were at least ten years old. These are some old servers that are stacked on a shelf, not a server rack, and only one of them is plugged in. The rest of them are sitting on a shelf, so they're not part of any server connectivity. I mean, I could understand if they were all bundled together and working to store stuff, but they weren't even plugged in. This one was, but it wasn't turned on. I asked him to turn it on and show me the software.

He turned this computer on, and I could immediately see that it was set up for a medical facility more than ten years prior. Mind you, it was the front screen, but there was nothing else on there. He couldn't do anything else with it; he couldn't load or go past that front-end screen; that was it.

I asked him to complete the tour with us, so he took me into a large room with a lot of writing on the whiteboard. Nothing had changed; it was still the same writing, dealing with the same software. And three of the same people were still there, studying and working to learn that software. But there was one significant difference this time: the name of the New York software company had been erased in the top corner, the original creator of the software. Now, the name of the big boss's company was handwritten on the whiteboard, the software that the big boss had claimed to be developing. When I confronted him with this little tidbit of information, he denied it completely and said this was his software. One of the ladies that was in the room studying the software kind of looked at me oddly. I explained to this gentleman that I had taken pictures the last time I was there and had photographs of the wall, and the name of the New York software firm was on the whiteboard at the time. He didn't respond to that.

We went back to his office to finish our conversation. I asked him to log on and show me the software that he was developing and running. He was able to pull up the front screen that had the graphics, logo, name, and label of his company that the immigrants were creating. I asked him to sign on for me. He couldn't open anything else. That was all that he had, his logo graphics. There was a sign on the screen with a basic design outline for the application and company. This hooked my curiosity. The big boss's company existed for five years. Big boss had petitioned for upwards of 100 people to come into the country, specifically to work on this software. In five years, with over 100 people, he had not accomplished anything but some graphics on his login screen. He explained that software development was a really difficult process and took a long time to do. Development often ran into years before it was accomplished.

I asked him, "How are you going to develop this software program when you farmed out **every** person that you've petitioned to work for other companies?"

He shrugged his shoulders and smiled at me. He didn't want to answer that. That would have put him on the spot and made his situation difficult.

I asked him again, and he wouldn't answer. This is one of the things you often run into. They don't answer because if they answer you and it's a lie, you can hold them accountable for that. If they don't answer, the best you can do is deny that application or petition.

As the reader, I want you to understand that this is common. I did hundreds of these. Every one of them was the same. It was the same patterns and routine **every** time. Generally, when I went out on these site visits, they were always a fraud or scam. There was something wrong with it. They were doing whatever they could to circumvent having to hire U.S. citizens to work.

The left and right-wing corporatists have always prided themselves on bringing in these poor workers to work for horrible wages. They've shifted that to the IT industry. Most of them don't care anything about any of these workers. I talked to the Department of Labor, and I'm telling you most of them don't care. I've talked to the immigration officer Service officers who work at the service centers where the employment petitions are approved. The DHS and USCIS does not care about the average American worker. I have had them show disdain for the workers. Not all, but enough to make a difference.

Bench Warmers

Another office practice that you see quite often is big boss companies will petition for large groups of these workers to enter the U.S. at the same time. In immigration, we have something we call benching; you see this all the time. Benching means they petitioned for that person to come in, but they don't have a job for them to do. They don't have anything in the house for them to work on. But they have a setup there so that those individuals can start immediately posting their resumes and looking on Indeed and other sites for companies that are trying to hire people. They have to go out and find their contracting job. Through the boss, immigrant companies and benching, they don't even need a job to enter the country, which is the antithesis of all immigration requirements. The other fast-track technique is where boss immigration companies bring you in and keep you in the bullpen (a type of benching) until there's an opening in their own company. They won't pay you. Immigrants wait until the job becomes available inside the company. One guy had been sitting in a company for six months waiting for a job. The immigrant had not been paid at all, so he looked for a job on his own. I don't know if his skill level was poor because it doesn't usually take that long under the system, but he had not been paid in months. Texas Service Center managed that company filing and did nothing to stop that company from continuing to do the same thing year after year.

After the Border

Field Of Dreams

I have barely scratched the surface of the employment scams. One last story to end all and to explain what I mean by "field of dreams." I was driving up to North Georgia to look for this IT Company. It was supposed to have about thirty immigrants working. They'd been petitioned to develop software, this new innovative purchasing software.

Oftentimes, when companies do these petitions, you do some basic research, even at the service center, and you get some red flags on the service. I don't want to say they're all bad. But when they googled this company and its address, they couldn't find the building. Mind you, this company had petitioned thirty people. Someone had finally decided to do a little more in-depth research on it. Because they couldn't find the building doesn't mean it's not there, right? You could do Google searches, and buildings were not there because of when the pictures were taken.

I drove up to this place. It's Gwinnett County, Georgia. This county is populous, but they still have a lot of country roads and a lot of fields and farms. I looked for this office for probably good hours to make sure I wasn't mistaken because there was nothing but fields there. And the address that was given to me was a big field. Grass and trees and no buildings. This company used several different addresses for a virtual office, which was about five miles down the road. I ended up calling the owner of the company and asking him about his employees.

And yes, the employee worked there. Yes, the employee was working in the office.

I explained that the office was a field. Without missing a beat, he says: "Well. We moved again." He claimed that he had moved about a mile down the road.

There was a small set of office buildings about a mile down the road. He said there were people there. Everybody was working.

When I got there, there was no one there. In that office and the two buildings beside it, there were people in there, and they said they've never seen anyone come and go out of that office ever. It'd been there for, you know, six months or so with no one ever entering or leaving. He rented a small office space out here in the country and left it there empty.

Guilty of Rape

When you hear stories about the border, especially illegal crossings on the border, there's even more going on than meets the television eye. I'll share a border case I worked on and anecdotal information from the field from other officers.

Early on in my career, I'd probably been with the service a year and a half, maybe two years, I had a gentleman come into my office with his attorney. This man was coming in for an **adjustment** of status interview. This was an employment-based interview. In other words, a company had petitioned for him to get permanent residence so he could work in America. We had a lot of Indian immigrants petitioning for high-tech jobs. Believe it or not, I also had many Indian petitioners for U.S. status who worked at Blimpie's sandwich shops, Subway sandwich shops, and dry cleaners. Small companies were constantly looking for fast food workers and laundry workers.

Here's an interesting twist to the way this program worked. In this story, a guy owned a Blimpie's sandwich shop, and his friend owned a Subway sandwich shop. What the two would do is the Subway owner would petition for the Blimpie's owner. Then the reverse: the guy who owned a Blimpie's would petition for Subway franchise owner. This would allow both to remain in America and **adjust** their status. Even though both sandwich shops were petitioning for workers in their stores, they were actually rival owners. In addition, the visitor visas of both sandwich shop owners expired a long time ago. The way the U.S. Immigration Service reconciled it was that companies were petitioning for people, not any particular individual, even though these two individuals owned their respective stores. It was a great loophole for immigrants with expired visas and small businesses. U.S. Immigration Service allows them to get away with it and angles like this all the time, even though neither one of the owners was a legal permanent resident, illegally in the country at that point. Lots of people were doing this. I went out on quite a few of these types of cases.

In this case, the one sandwich shop owner was an older gentleman in his sixties. He looked a little decrepit and walked with a cane. He had really serious acne on his face. He looked like he had a pretty rough life. I don't know what was going on with him, but he didn't look well. When the sandwich shop owner came to the office, he always came with his attorney. The owner was married and had children, but no one came with him to the office. Kind of strange. He lived in a country town deep in South Georgia, probably two hours south of Atlanta.

The reason I mentioned this shop owner is because we do background checks, and as I looked through his background check, I noted that he had been arrested before. In this case, he had been arrested for raping a young woman in California. This sandwich guy had been prosecuted, convicted, and sent to prison for rape.

He had served his time. As is most cases with aggravated (AG) felons, once his time was up, enforcement and removal gathered him up and sent him back to India.

Sometime after that, he managed to work his way back to Mexico. The sandwich shop owner's story (now a common one) was that he went to Mexico and crossed the border illegally into the United States. Usually, when they come across the border illegally, they're not eligible for adjustment. But this man fell under a "sunset" period. Sunset essentially meant that if you entered the U.S. before December of 2000 and filed your paperwork before April of 2001, then you were eligible for adjustment of status if you had something pending before April 30th of 2001. Shockingly, the shop owner had all that, and he had employment. The employment status filing and certification (Form ETA-750A) ran through the Department of Labor. And it was one of those cases where he had his own shop, and he was actually being paid. Yeah, he was actually being petitioned for by another shop owner. I interviewed him, and I began to talk to him about his conviction and charges. This was a story I got quite often from people who were convicted of crimes. In this case, he said, "Oh, I didn't rape anyone, that was my twin brother."

You'll hear this routine quite often. A lot of times, the petitioner will blame it on a relative, usually on the brother, who's most likely fictitious. Well, this guy said that he had a twin brother who was the rapist. As an immigration officer, you ask yourself if that is possible or plausible. Sure, it's possible; however, the fingerprint evidence we were aware of showed that he was the criminal.

I needed to verify some things, so I asked this shop owner to provide his own criminal court records. I gave him a letter telling him to come back in four weeks for further discussion, records investigation, and to make sure he had everything correct.

He came back in, and I began to interview him again. One of the things I noted was that he came again only with his attorney. He was in the lobby by himself. It was an empty day at work. There wasn't anyone else in the lobby, and it was the end of the workday. Seeing him outside with no one around me, it dawned on me the shop owner has a wife and adult daughter. And he had said that his daughter needed some help, not that she was physically ill or anything, but she was his daughter. I don't know how he was able to get around. It might have been a front, I don't know. I had to go based on the sandwich owner using a cane and looking fairly decrepit, walking slowly and hunched over. To make sure they can survive and live. But the suspicious thing was no one ever came with him. Usually, in immigration, if you have a wife and kid, they'll be in the lobby or say hi. He looked in bad shape, and even his attorney kept saying that he was in really rough shape; he wouldn't strike you as a person who could help anyone. Someone always comes to support and guide you through the process, but he always came by himself, and that's not a question we can ask.

I remember I got some information back on him. We (immigration officers) organized his file and also did some other checks to make sure everything was clean since his prison term ended. When he came back, I talked to him some more. We had his fingerprints on file, as I mentioned.

We had both the criminal fingerprints in the file from his booking and prison term and his immigration fingerprints. Back then, we were still doing actual ink prints with a blue card. We fingerprinted him again—reprinted him. I had one of the fingerprint experts go back and review all the data, prints, and files; although I've been trained in reading fingerprints, I thought it was a good idea to get an expert. Today, they don't train U.S. immigration officers in fingerprinting. Both the expert and I agreed that the sandwich shop owner was the same person as the convicted felon in California. His fingerprints matched what was on file and reprints.

So I had to explain to the shop owner that regardless of whether or not he had a twin brother, his twin brother's fingerprints would not match his fingerprints. There'd be enough difference in them that we could see. I told the shop owner I needed to step out of the room for a few minutes and confirm with someone else. So I left him in the interview room; however, I didn't really go confer with anyone else. I walked out and stood in the hall, just to the side of the room where he couldn't see me. The shop owner's and attorney's backs were toward me, so they couldn't see me.

I was able to observe the sandwich shop owner as he leaned over to his attorney and said loud enough for me to hear, "I should have never admitted to that rape." He did not know I was standing there. So he basically admitted the rape to his attorney.

That's when I turned around, walked back into the room, and said, "So you did admit to the rape before. You were convicted, and you spent time in prison," and that was the end of that case. Both he and the attorney were a bit shocked I had overheard them.

That being said, he was screwed. I called criminal investigations across the hall at the end of the interview. In the process, I denied the sandwich ship owner's application for **adjustment** because he was an aggravated felon. Immigration investigations came across the hall, handcuffed him, walked him back across the hallway, and processed him for removal again.

Difficult Moments

I worked for U.S. Immigration in various positions and locations for twenty years. I spent most of my time in the Atlanta office. I did a brief stint in Washington, DC, working on national security cases. I worked in Birmingham, Alabama, for brief snippets. I also worked at the Fingerprint Centers. I was assigned to the Homeland Security Investigations for four years.

In Atlanta, I ran the gambit. I was an Adjudications Officer interviewing people for adjustment of status, applications to become citizens, adoptees, and employment-based applications.

I also worked around naturalization, people who became U.S. citizens, conducting ceremonies, and doing other aspects of that interviewing, making sure they're eligible. As a supervisor, I would conduct immigration naturalization ceremonies throughout the states of Georgia and Alabama. I also did naturalizations for soldiers who were going through the Fort Benning Immigrant Programs in Columbus, Georgia.

I finished my time in Atlanta, as I said before, doing Fraud Detection and National Security (FDNS). Several issues occur when you live and work in the same area for that many years.

1) You're going to be accused of many things, many wrongdoings, whether you do it or not. You must understand that people are desperate. People want to stay in the United States. And you will be questioned and accused of things. And they'll stick by their answers.

2) You're going to run into people who you may have met before working in immigration. You're going to meet people who later will come in for immigration purposes. You're going to know friends who are going through the immigration process and families who are going through the immigration process. So, twenty years allows a lot of people to cross your path inside and outside of the office.

3) When people find out that you work for U.S. Immigration, they are going to ask you for advice and ask you to help them. Some of them might even be friends or family members, and you must be firm because you can't give them special treatment. I was adamant about drawing the ethical line as a U.S. immigration officer.

When I became a fraud officer, it became a little more startling and alarming. It's much more serious. You're doing investigations of fraudulent activity; you're in the middle of it.

If you live in a community that has a large immigrant population, you're going to see a lot of people. I've gotten used to some of it. I've gotten used to people yelling at me in the office because I denied them, or any number of things, accusations that might occur in the process of doing my job. People sometimes are angry; I mean, this is their life that you're dealing with, and when you must tell them bad news, they don't necessarily take it that well.

After being a fraud officer for several years, those types of issues became a little more frequent. Some of the encounters became a little more concerning. A couple of situations occurred that were alarming. I interviewed a gentleman one week. That weekend, I was in the Home Depot near my house. This gentleman worked in the Home Depot. He was a West African. As I was walking through Home Depot, I kept hearing this little *Psssst* sound. I didn't know where this was coming from at first, but then this little gentleman peeked out around the corner of one of the aisles. He said, "Officer Lee. Do you remember me?"

I did remember him, and I remembered that I had talked to him and interviewed him and his wife that prior week. I discovered that their marriage was not valid and that the Home Depot guy was in a fraudulent marriage.

He was trying to explain to me in the middle of Home Depot how he was going to get his documents together. He needed to prove his marriage was good. He was sure I would change my mind.

I explained to him that I was not on the clock and that I was walking through Home Depot to get some supplies. I didn't feel comfortable discussing his immigration case in the middle of Home Depot. He wanted to keep talking to me about it. I finally had to cut him off and say, "Look, I'm not discussing this with you here in the middle of the store."

Not even two weeks later, I interviewed a gentleman in my office based on a possible fraudulent marriage. Through my investigation, I found that his claimed U.S. citizen wife and marriage wasn't true. They didn't live in an apartment together; they had submitted some fake documents to us. It was another one of the many fraudulent cases that I've done related to the *Operation: Courthouse Steps*. But I do recall this gentleman had a serious fraudulent marriage, and there were a lot of major issues. There were even some issues of bank fraud and financial fraud within this gentleman's file.

That's not what bothered me. What bothered me is my son had an open house at his school that evening. My wife, my daughter, my son. We all went to school together. It's the beginning of the school year, so you go to each one of the classes, meet and greet all the teachers, and prepare for what's going to happen in the next school year. As I'm walking down the hall in my son's school, this same gentleman is standing in the hall. He is there with his children. He is also there with a woman who is not the woman he had brought into my office earlier in the morning.

Mind you, I am not on the clock. I am with my wife and my children. He is standing in the hall. There's another woman with his children. The kids are calling him Daddy. He looks at me, smiles, and shrugs his shoulders. I did remember that when I interviewed him earlier that day, he had not told me of any children or another woman in his life. But what was alarming is that he was the parent of the kids going to school with my son. Off-campus encounters didn't happen all the time, but it was becoming more frequent, hitting too close to home, as the expression goes.

Because I have done so many interviews and cases, thousands of them, I knew that my name was in the DeKalb County community. People kind of expected to see me when I did a site visit to a residence.

Sometimes, I would see an immigrant who had already become a naturalized U.S. citizen returning to the immigration office to fill out paperwork for a spouse from their home country. When I'd meet the person again, we were both familiar, and they might say, "I was wondering when you were going to get around to my file." They knew my name. They knew what I was doing within the process.

VOODOO Curse

One day, a Homeland Security Special Agent reached out to me. One of the gentlemen who had been in for an immigration status change was part of a marriage fraud scheme. The HSI Agent told me the immigrant was attempting to travel outside of the country with many electronics, TVs, and computers to take them back home to Nigeria. Some type of fencing racket featuring the resale of electronics.

There were red flags out on this fencing guy. He was a serious player in financial fraud and bank fraud. Homeland Security Investigation's Agent and I went to the apartment where the fencing guy claimed to live. This was supposed to be the house where he and his claimed U.S. citizen spouse resided.

As I said, there were a lot of flags. The fencing guy had a lot of identities, passports, U.S. driver's licenses, foreign driver's licenses, and things of that nature sent to this apartment. The U.S. government has agreements all over the world to kind of keep an eye on fake IDs to help mitigate some of the financial fraud and identity fraud that goes on throughout the world. This gentleman had been flagged in another country because of his mail that was bound for the United States. And the postal inspectors in that country had caught on to a large number of passports being shipped to his address in the United States.

When we arrived at the apartment, we introduced ourselves and knocked on the door; two Nigerian gentlemen were in the apartment. They were involved in financial fraud with the gentleman. The HSI agent that I was with had information on the two Nigerian guys holding multiple identifications.

217

The HSI agent asked to go through one of the Nigerian guys' wallets, and he complied. In the wallet, he had several different photo IDs with different names on them. He also had different credit cards with different names. The problem was the small West African criminal element was organized and in some cases, supported by corrupt home government officials.

We talked to these two Nigerian gentlemen for a while about the fencing guy we were looking for. There was a car in the apartment parking lot that belonged to the fencing guy. One of the guys in the apartment said that he used the car and that he drove it around, and was borrowing it. He stated that the fencing guy permitted him to use the car.

There was a Georgia Department of Driver Services Agent with us on the site visit. He and I walked down to the car. He looked at the car windows, and one of the things he noted was an envelope on the floor in the car.

We got permission from the Nigerian gentleman, who then opened the door for the Georgia agent so he could look through the car. The Nigerian also opened the trunk. In the backseat was a brown manila envelope. I pointed it out to the Georgia agent, and he pulled it out. There were lots of checks for thousands of dollars in different names. Names of people the HSI Special Agent had been looking for. In the front of the car, The Georgia Agent looked through the glove box and found $7,000 in cash.

When he went through the trunk of the car, he found checks that had not been cashed yet and even checks that had already been cashed. More identities. We're talking about thousands and thousands of dollars in this car, in envelopes, laying on the backseat, and lying in the trunk of the car. The case grew into a major financial fraud cornucopia.

We didn't find the guy that we were looking for at the apartment. Even though we couldn't find him at home, the fencing guy was obviously busy with any type of crime you could think of. The HIS Special Agent calls the fencing guy directly and sets up a meeting to meet with him the next day. The fencing guy answered the phone, and he agreed to meet us at a restaurant near his apartment the next day. He gave us the address of the second apartment. When we arrive, we find more Nigerian henchmen living in the second apartment.

Still, there's no sign of the fencing guy anywhere, and we still haven't found his U.S. citizen spouse. I do, however, have information on her, and I have an idea of where she may live. Since we can't find him, we decide to go and see if we can find his wife. We drove to her home not far away, still in the same county and city. We knocked on the door, and the fencing guy's claimed U.S. citizen spouse answered the door. She told us that she hadn't seen fencing up in months and that she knew he had a girlfriend. She wasn't even sure exactly where he lived. She did admit to the fact that she married him to help him get immigration benefits. She stated the car sitting in the driveway was the car that the fencing guy gave her for marrying him. She was irritated by this lousy car. This car was a salvage car. It had been either a hurricane flood or some type of flooding. There were other mechanical issues with the car, to such an extent that she could not get the car registered or use it to drive on the roads.

One of the things I note repeatedly is: People get involved in these marriages and think that it's going to be easy and good money. But if you're dealing with people who are already willing to commit fraud and manipulate the system, you must understand that they're willing to do the same thing to you. I've never seen anyone get a real benefit out of marrying someone for immigration benefits. The only people who succeed are the people at the top and the people in the middle who arrange marriages and get money from the immigrants. Not the $500 here and there from the actors in the fraudulent marriage sham.

We ended up meeting with the fencing guy the next day at the local restaurant. We think that he's going to drive up to the restaurant, and you're going to see him and know what kind of car he drives and all of that. We waited in the parking lot, and he came walking up from down the street to the restaurant. He doesn't want us to see what kind of car he drives or where he comes from. Fortunately, we had someone watching out for that, and they were able to spot his car a couple of parking lots down and see where he came from.

For me, this meeting isn't lucrative. It isn't lucrative for the investigators, either. You run into this where sometimes they're arrogant, and they think you don't have anything on them. So, they can be a little difficult and snippy with you. In this case, this fencing guy was that way. He was short and curt. And he was not going to give up any information.

We ended up leaving this meeting not much better off than when we came in. The fencing guy didn't give us enough information with details of him lying. We didn't get him to make any confessions. I think the HSI agent doing the criminal side of the case had sufficient evidence to do some damage to him. I had enough information that I think we could deny his marriage and let that go.

I ended up getting a phone call and being called into the office. I wasn't sure what it was about at first. But when I got in, they sat me down with my supervisor and the HSI Agent that had gone out with me. I was told the fencing guy had been attempting to fly out of the country and had been stopped by U.S. Customs and Border Patrol or Protection (CBP) at the airport. When CBP went through his phone, they found a lot of text messages. The fencing guy was mentioning a problem that he had. He was texting someone in Nigeria that was the head guy or kingpin for this criminal enterprise.

One of the texts started with ... they were having a problem. And they needed somehow to resolve this problem. The problem was me and the HSI special agent that I had gone out and talked to the fencing guy with. The HSI agent was doing the financial fraud side of it. They were trying to figure out how they would get rid of the problem. Or should I say problems? This set off a lot of alarm bells and whistles. There were concerns the kingpin of the fencing guy's operation was putting a hit out on us.

They assigned another special agent to go out and try to find this guy as quickly as they could. I was kind of locked down in the office.

Eventually, they did let me read some of the texts that were being passed around some of the questions, and some of the stuff that was going on. After reading them, I became a little less alarmed about what was happening.

The kingpin in Nigeria sent the fencing guy a voodoo curse to put on us. He had spelled out all the items that he needed to make the curse so that we would go away. There was a list of items, and I don't remember everything. But it was some type of vegetation, it was some plants. There was an antelope head involved. I don't remember all the things, but it was a list of ten or fifteen items that were needed for the voodoo curse to work. I don't remember if there was an incantation or what it was, but the kingpin did give the recipe of what needed to be done for the curse and how to mix the items.

For a long time, I laughed about this and said that, apparently, it didn't work because I didn't go away. But I'm not so sure today that the voodoo curse didn't work on us. The HSI special agent and I both ended up retiring. Because of this and all the other concerns I had, I ended up leaving the Atlanta office and going to FLETC (Federal Law Enforcement Training Center) Charleston to be an instructor. I don't know if I can laugh at it anymore. It must have worked.

Conclusion

My twenty-year journey at the INS and USCIS as an officer, supervisor, and trainee was the greatest privilege of my life. Every day, I found new worlds and cultures right here in the USA and connected to countries the emigrants traveled from. I have so many great memories and friends from serving with the fine officers and agents at USCIS and all throughout DHS and the State Department. I'd like to thank the reader for allowing me to share these memories.

My greatest and warmest feeling was swearing in the new immigrants. I represented America, Freedom, and Lady Liberty (The Aura of the Statue of Liberty); I saw the joy of immigrants who went through a long journey of both distance and perseverance to join us in the USA to be part of our unique family. We all know for various reasons that America is on its worst days … it was nice to see America's finest moment, the swearing-in of new naturalized citizens.

I hope you have a sense of some of my experiences as a U.S. immigration officer. Even though I covered many flaws in U.S. immigration,

The stories in this book may not seem like an immediate threat to national security; however, they all chip away at the foundation of America and over time impact our national security. They also impact our financial systems, our American structure, and our safety.

I've identified some of the immigration problems in this book. What are the solutions to the problems? I wish I had a simple answer that would appease everyone's sensibilities and work for everyone on a constitutional and political level.

After years in U.S. immigration, I realized that one side's political solution is going to be extremely offensive to the other. We are so polarized today that you cannot come to some common ground or some understanding, and there are many third-party political groups with definitive positions on immigration as well. In addition, some associations, nonprofits supporting immigrants, and others in the industry want nothing to do with enforcement.

Here are my solutions, and at the end, I'll bullet point legislation.

Immigration Attorneys. When I first started, some seriously good immigration attorneys were both advocates for their immigrants but also would not tolerate any illegal or procedural misconduct. Immigrants who defrauded the system, cheated the system, or did anything nefarious found it difficult to find quality attorneys to represent them. Somewhere along the lines, that changed, a lot of those attorneys retired. That doesn't mean all of them were good. There were some nasty attorneys that I dealt with who were just devious and deceptive.

Now, most attorneys and most participants in immigration lawyer groups like the American Immigration Lawyers Association (AILA) advocate for finding any way to get immigrants into the country. It's almost a false sense of heroism, equating open borders with the great historical efforts of the Underground Railroad during the horrors of slavery. There's no correlation at all. In U.S. Immigration, we openly want immigrants into the country and process nearly 100,000 per month; however, it's our job to vet incoming immigrants for criminal activity and follow the rules set forth by Congress and signed into law. Those laws were heavily debated by elected officials and signed by a president. To circumvent the law and Constitution in the name of faux historical nobility is a decoupling from reality.

Choose a number and stick to it. We have to decide how many immigrants we want to come into this country a year. I always place the number of two million immigrants per year coming into the country legally. Make sure there's a legal system for about two million people to come into this country. We can most likely absorb that number without difficulty.

Eric Bolling, conservative businessman and former host of Fox News program *The Five* explained on his show that he would be comfortable with four million legal immigrants per year. This is one of many examples of leeway for multi-party and ideological agreements for a new immigration plan.

The U.S. Border Patrol frequently says thirty percent of immigrant women get raped trying to cross into the U.S., so a plan must be put into place to stop this immediately. In addition, Fentanyl is killing our youth on a mass scale.

Immigration policy for everyone. The immigration system should be open to everyone. I'm not a fan of a system that only allows the "upper echelon" and the most educated to come here; inversely, I'm not a fan of a system that just lets poor people come here either. The system should be open to both; we need the entire spectrum of wealth and education. People who are struggling to come here will bring their energy and drive to be successful, and we need people who are educated as well, so it should be an open system and equal opportunity.

Global diversity system. I'm a fan of the old diversity system. There were some flaws in it. There was some fraud. We could work out those kinks. But I like the idea of a diversity system for the whole world. A diversity system sets up some people from each country for entry into the U.S., Not just countries that are under-represented, but the whole world. Let's say you divide that by a country's population, and you give them a certain number of people who can come here per year.

The diversity program would have to be offset by some marriage petitions and applications. But regardless of whether you marry someone or not, you're limited to two million people per year. So if you get married, and your wife and husband don't make it the first year, maybe you give them the head of the line the next year to come in. But you only bring in two million people per year as immigrants.

Enforcement. There are between twenty and thirty million illegal immigrants in this country, contrary to what the government tells you, eleven million. They're lying to you.

How do I come to that number? Between one and a half million and two million people a year come into this country illegally, mainly crossing the southern border. There's no way to adjust their status legally. And they do not leave, and we do not deport them or remove them. From the time I went to work with U.S. immigration in 2002 until the time I retired in 2022, that's twenty years. Even if you said during that time frame, a million people came here illegally, that's still nearly twenty million people. Prior to my work for immigration, there were seven different amnesties. Each one allowed illegal increased the number of people coming illegally or overstaying their visas.

a) **The wall.** Will is more important than a wall. If migrants want to enter illegally into the U.S. and know there are no penalties for breaking laws, overstaying, or illegal entry with no chance of deportation, then no wall, steel slat border wall, smart wall, surveillance technologies, drones, vehicles and increased number of border agents will stop the flow. Sure, a wall will stop a rush at the border. President Clinton famously built a wall out of old Vietnam steel airport runway components at the San Diego/Tijuana port of entry, and just a few years back, President Trump had his lengthier Wall as well. The Border Patrol asked for strategic barriers for less than 500 miles at hot spots. Any amount of wall or barriers doesn't matter; the migrants will just go around it, climb over, or cut through the wall. Even more, just enter a POE (port of entry) with a friendly administration, and that friendly administration will just let everyone in or find an excuse to let everyone in to the USA. I hate to disappoint the creative gentleman that wore a hilarious and fun "border wall suit" to President Trump rallies, but I have to communicate the best ways to allocate resources and deterrents.

b) **Airports' higher percentage**. More illegal entry comes through the airports than across the Rio Grande. Senator Rubio emphasized this in several TV interviews. The people who fly in become illegal when they overstay their visas. They're permitted a period of stay.

c) **Overstaying your welcome.** Illegal immigrant figures do not include the number of people who come here as B1-B2 visitors, exchange students, and various other means. They overstay their visa and never go home. Fifty million-plus people legally cross our borders each year. Many of those are visitors who come into this country and do not leave; again, it's due to lack of enforcement and common knowledge of the government's inability to punish, thus, no consequences. Looking at the numbers, between three and five percent of those visitors never leave the country. That's another 1.5 million people. Even if we said 1.1 million people over the same period, that's another 19 million people. Now, a lot of those people do adjust their status and become legal permanent residents. Not all of them, but a big chunk of them do. So, I have to set that straight. It just is what you have to understand.

d) **To be or not to amnesty.** This was the famous repartee between Senator Cruz and Rubio in the presidential primaries in 2016. What's amnesty, what should be done, who's tough, whose not? What to do about the tens of millions of illegal immigrants here already? President Eisenhower rounded up over a million Mexicans and sent them back to Mexico on buses and ships. That hurt labor markets and gave such a bad vibe that President Eisenhower created the concept of a day labor pass to augment the feelings and labor shortage. Since we can never deport twenty to thirty million illegal immigrants in this country, we have to figure out a way and a rule that allows them to stay to some degree while getting a good handle on who's here illegally. And there needs to be consequences for the fact that immigrants either entered the country illegally or they came here on a visa and overstayed illegally. Plus, those consequences should be a message to others that coming here will not benefit them.

Strict penalties for illegal entry, overstaying, and/or falsification of records. Many visitors to the USA on B1 or B2 visitor visas overstay. In the view of the law, their status becomes illegal. A common circumventing of the law is students on F1 visas never going to school here.

In a deterrent and functional immigration system, overstayers would not benefit from the fraud or misuse of status; however, that's not the case, so they stay and the vast majority of the time are never held accountable.

The solution? Get tough, and this includes both the overstayers and DACA program recipients.

The overstaying immigrants should not be granted either legal permanent residence or U.S. citizenship. Instead, we give them a status akin to the DACA program, deferred action for arriving aliens. What this essentially means is these individuals would be able to live here, would be able to work here, and would be able to raise a family here even though they ignored their obligations under U.S. law.

To be given a second chance, overstayers, and DACA would have to sign a conditional waving of all trial rights. This probationary period would last the entire time they are here, even if it's a lifetime. Surprisingly, there's a lot of middle ground for comprehensive immigration reform. Popular conservative talk show host Rush Limbaugh (who passed on in 2021) said on the radio and TV that he would be for amnesty with a twenty-five-year ban on voting for the violators. Years later, he reduced it to an approximately fifteen-year ban on voting.

My suggested rules in the lifetime probationary period for expanded DACA amnesty seekers: If at any time overstayers and DACA recipients commit any crime that is significant, such as multiple DUIs, shoplifting, or any number of crimes, we should send them home. U.S. Immigration has a slew of listed criminal activities that could remove the overstayers and DACA recipients from the country immediately, aggravated felonies. The fact that we let you overstay and granted you deferred action requires the overstayers and DACA to give up their rights to immigration proceedings like the visa waiver programs. To be able to stay here and work here legally, you will agree to immediate removal; if arrested without a hearing, you will agree to get on a plane, you will agree to pay your way to fly out of this country, and you will go home, and that will be it. We won't waste time or get bogged down with the system for those people who have already committed the first crime of illegally entering the country or overstaying and turn around and committed a second one …

The reaction to my policy suggestion may be contrary to what political attorneys will tell you; however, I've worked within the community of immigrants, and I've known advocates for immigrants; they often agree with this method and are even accepting of this. This is something they would agree to since most are just decent people. But they could never get the benefit to a higher status, their children can enjoy citizenship. They should not be granted that full faith in the system where they are made legal permanent residents or U.S. citizens because that has enormous value, and they cheated the line to get it. Rewarding "jumping in front of the line" with legal permanent residence or citizenship gives them too much privilege and undeserved reward.

Undercutting industry standard wages. We must strengthen the laws against employment-based fraud. Certain small companies and large corporations circumvent every system they can to make sure they don't have to hire U.S. citizens. All businesses with more than twelve employees are required to e-verify and document their results. Also, we must make realistic employment pricing. What I mean by that is that we've got to be realistic about how much a new immigrant gets paid versus a U.S. citizen. For instance, in the IT industry, nobody pays anyone $65,000 a year who has five years of experience in computer software engineering, that's way below the market value. That is just not going to happen, but we allow businesses to pretend that's industry-standard wages and pay newly arrived immigrant visa petitioners H1-B that low of wage.

For example, unscrupulous CEOs linked to H1-B scams will create a company called "Acme Internet Services" or some such name. The CEO will be caught committing fraud with one person, two people, and three people. Well, the USCIS doesn't ban or bar Acme Internet Services from ever petitioning for anyone else. They could petition next year for someone else. Acme should be barred from petitioning people ever again.

The CEO, as an individual, should be banned from ever petitioning another employee, regardless of the company. This type of activity is associated with entire families in the U.S. that post scamming companies; therefore, family members associated with the fraudster CEO should also be banned if linked to the process.

Marriage fraud. Marriage fraud is a complex issue within the U.S. Immigration Service. It is far more rampant than anyone within the hierarchy of immigration or the officers or agents who work at the service centers want to admit. The boots on the ground, the people on the front lines understand this. The people in the offices where you interview potential marriages understand this. The problem is defining marriage fraud and making that determination. Shockingly, as an immigration officer, I am unable to make a determination of marriage fraud. The rules are strict. They're very difficult. They're very conflicted on what constitutes marriage fraud or how you determine marriage fraud. An immigration officer is unable to do that for the most part. U.S. Immigration Services will tell you the officers make the determination, but that's not true. The way you actually determine marriage fraud is a judge has to determine it, meaning you have to take them to an immigration judge, but as a U.S. immigration officer, you can't initiate. It's very difficult to take a single scheme marriage fraud case to court in major cities like Atlanta. An immigration judge has to make a determination that marriage fraud existed. In some cases, if both the immigrant and the U.S. citizen admit to the fraud, that is sufficient. But no one in their right mind would admit to the fraud. The problem with the immigration judges is most of them, in the last few years, have been hired by extremely radical leftists, and they are unwilling to say that marriage fraud occurred, no matter what the circumstance. No matter what you find or discover, the radical judges are just not going to do it because, in their ideology, it's too harsh of a punishment not to let everyone into the country. According to the actual law, immigrants are barred for life from becoming an immigrant to this country for committing marriage fraud.

So we must find a way to make it stick, not necessarily easier to determine that marriage fraud exists but to codify it in some way that it's more acceptable when an immigration officer has found sufficient evidence. Give the U.S. immigration officers initial judgement and final authority, then if an immigrant challenges an officer's ruling, file an appeal with the appellate courts, who can then overturn it. Do not allow immigration judges to make the initial judgment.

Just to give you an idea and understanding, here's the best I can do as a U.S. immigration officer after investigating a marriage: even if I find that they submitted fraudulent lease agreements, fraudulent insurance records, fake documents to create a charade that the marriage is real, even if all of their documents aren't real, I still can't stop the marriage as long as they haven't verbally lied to me. They've never lived together, resided together, they've never consummated the marriage (slept together). They don't even really know each other. It's nearly impossible for me to stop the marriage from going through. Since I can't determine it's a fraud under those restrictions, a political immigration judge certainly won't determine that it was a marriage fraud. Add to that, if I put the couple in proceedings in front of an immigration judge, it will take me five years to get a hearing. In the meantime, the ninety-day fiancée becomes a 1,826-day fiancée.

Deportation. Television and movies show a majority of America's impression of deportation goes like this … when an immigrant is in front of a federal judge and ruled to be deported, they are handcuffed, whisked away in a bus, tossed over the border, and the guards yell, "Never come back." Let me tell you that never happens. Here's why.

First of all, immigration judges are administrative judges, meaning they serve at the whim of the executive branch.

We have to figure out a way to streamline the deportation process. As I said above, it takes five years or more to get someone removed from this country. From the moment they were in proceedings until the time they saw an immigration judge was over five years. When needing to stall, immigration attorneys ask for extensions and usually get an extension from the judge. This will extend the process for another year. Often, the immigrant will marry a U.S. citizen and file a visa petition. This is supposedly frowned upon and supposedly taboo. But most officers ignore this and still grant permission to stay. Judges have no jurisdiction over I-130 petitions. The judge should say, "No, I don't care that you filed an I-130 while you're in proceedings. It doesn't count here. I'm still removing you, and you can have that adjudicated while you're overseas." In reality, the judge will always remand the case file back to the USCIS and let them decide the next procedural step.

If a judge miraculously finds an immigrant to be deportable under the Immigration Nationality Act, the immigrant can appeal to the BIA (Board of Immigration Appeals), so it will take another few years before you get removed from this country. I've seen it take ten years or more to get someone removed. So, when you think that people are removed fast and whisked away, that is not true.

Removals used to happen at the airports, but that was not really deportation. That was just because the immigrants were caught at the airports; the immigration officers didn't determine that they were not eligible to stay. So, the immigrant was placed on a plane back home. The immigrant was not even deported, just sent home. They could come back in a week and potentially be let in. Even this does not happen today. Removals should be brought back and used liberally by Customs and Border Patrol.

I think we need more qualified and nonpolitical judges. We need a better and streamlined immigration process. When an immigrant is ordered deported, they could have a review immediately by a panel of judges. You could do that within the same week. Judges would just look at the single judge's decision, reviewing it as you would a supervisor's. Was the decision sound? Was it based on law supported by facts? If so, then the immigrant goes home. The immigrant stays in detention until they leave.

My Immigration Solutions After Working at USCIS for 20 Years

1) Expanded DACA (Deferred Action Childhood Arrivals) becomes a fourth type of probationary status other than visa holder, permanent resident (green card), and naturalized citizen. All immigrants with illegal status currently in the country will receive Amnesty under the DACA program.

2) Any overstayers of Visas like students, diplomats, or H1-B, B-1/B-2 holders will also have a status of illegal and in order to stay, must agree to the lifetime probationary Expanded DACA Policy.

3) Any immigrant who enters the country after the signing of Expanded DACA will not be the beneficiary of any benefit. They must return to their home country.

4) Amnesty DACA recipients will never be allowed to become permanent residents and/or naturalized citizens. You will never be allowed to vote in a federal election.

5) Amnesty DACA recipients will not be allowed to petition for family members outside of the country.

6) Any Expanded DACA recipient that is convicted of a significant crime or an aggravated felony will be immediately deported without an immigration hearing. You waive your rights to due process and a hearing by becoming a DACA Amnesty Status recipient. Significant crimes determined by the courts are three DUIs, robbery, domestic violence, etc.

7) If you don't like these conditions, you can leave the country. Wait outside of the country for a year, then go to the back of the line behind all others waiting to get into the country legally and start the process over for a green card and potentially becoming a naturalized citizen.

8) CEOs, as individuals, and their companies should be banned from ever petitioning another immigrant H1-B employee, regardless of the company, if they are caught abusing the system or running H-1B immigration mills.

9) The maximum number of new immigrants per year is two million.

10) Expanded DACA recipients will have to file back taxes; however, no DACA recipients will be entitled to any monies from refunds, including the aggregate monies owed or refunded in all years required to file back taxes. Court decisions are coming down as the book is being written.

11) Congress authorizes the use of military force by the President of the United States against any terrorist cartel that engages in systematic mass rape, human trafficking, or distribution of Fentanyl (or illegal drugs of similar toxicity).

12) All U.S. businesses over twelve employees are required to e-verify, document and archive their search records.

13) New immigrant H1-B arrivals in IT cannot receive wages more than ten percent below industry marketplace standards.

14) After a deportation judgement of a non-expanded DACA recipient, allow only one week for an appeal from a three-judge panel. The immigrant is detained for a week and sent to the country of origin if the judge panel rules against the immigrant. Deported Expanded DACA recipients will not have this privilege.

Immigration is complicated. These suggestions do not solve all the problems, just a few of the major ones. But constantly kicking the can down the road, leaving the borders open, and sending mixed messages to keep Homeland Security in a constant state of confusion. Jumping from one crisis to another will only exasperate the problem. In my twenty years of service, nothing has been solved, it just gets worse.

The right champions moral wars and strict prosecution of laws; however, cartels haven't been bombed like other foreign countries halfway around the world, and cartel sex trafficking leaders haven't been extracted or rendered on a mass scale like El Chapo. The left's foundation is the protection of women's rights; who's championing the rape victims, whose trying to stop it? Each major party just blames the other, a *Get out of Jail Free* card for politicians ducking the issue.

Biography

My name is Richard Lee. I was a U.S. immigration officer for twenty years. I also served eight years in the U.S. Coast Guard and two years working for Senator Richard Shelby. I am married with three wonderful children.

After graduation from the Federal Law Enforcement Training Center (FLETC) basic training, I was stationed back in Atlanta. I spent seventeen years as an adjudication officer/immigration service officer (AO/ISO).

I then trained new immigration officers for FDNS and Basic Immigration Service Officers at the FLETC in Charleston, South Carolina. I taught fraud, fraud detection, national security, interviewing techniques, and how to conduct site visits, along with writing reports.

My final position with USCIS (U.S. Citizenship and Immigration Services) was at the FLETC in Charleston. I'd always dreamt of being an instructor and going to FLETC full-time. I thought it was where I would probably end my career.

I really enjoyed being in the classroom. I enjoyed teaching, but none of that seemed to be working out for me, especially with the natural restrictions of video conferencing as opposed to actual in person classes. Some personal family issues were going on, and I thought it best to retire and focus on my family. I spoke to my wife, and it seemed like the best thing to do. I retired on June 30th, 2022.

After a few months of retirement, I decided to write this book, but I wanted to do it in a unique way. I wanted to tell the stories of my career … real stories, not like a traditional book. I grabbed a digital recorder and spoke into the mic, telling my story and the story of American immigration as if the reader and I were sitting around a campfire or having a couple of beers at a local pub.

Made in United States
Orlando, FL
13 February 2024

43667618R00134